starting with
rhyme

Action rhyme activities
for early years

Irene Yates

Author
Irene Yates

Editor
Jane Bishop

Assistant editor
Sally Gray

Series designer
Joy White

Designer
Louise Belcher

Illustrations
James Alexander

Cover
Lynda Murray

Designed using Aldus Pagemaker
Processed by Scholastic Ltd, Leamington Spa
Printed in Great Britain by Hartnolls Ltd, Bodmin

Published by Scholastic Ltd, Villiers House, Clarendon Avenue,
Leamington Spa, Warwickshire CV32 5PR

© 1997 Scholastic Ltd Text © 1997
1 2 3 4 5 6 7 8 9   7 8 9 0 1 2 3 4 5

British Library Cataloguing-in-Publication Data
A catalogue record for this book is available from the British Library.

ISBN 0-590-53657-5

Contents

Introduction 5

chapter one

I'm a little teapot

Introduction 7
Make a teapot book 8
Post in the pot 9
Mugs and spoons 10
Match the teapots 11
Add some water 12
Cups and saucers 13
This is the way 14
Place the teapot 15
Pretty pot patterns 16
Sounds like 17
Pottery shapes 18
Invite a friend 19
Come to our tea-party 20
How many? 21
Baby pizzas 22

chapter two

Here we go round the mulberry bush

Introduction 23
Whether the weather 24
Jack Frost 25
Look at leaves 26

How many berries? 27
Can you do this? 28
Sew-a-bush 29
What if ...? 30
Bush, tree, hedge 31
Forest picture 32
Weather sounds 33
How shall we go? 34
Good to know 35
Cold and frosty morning 36
Round the mulberry bush 37
Frosty bushes 38

chapter three

Pat-a-cake

Introduction 39
What can we buy? 40
Who for? 41
Match the cake 42
How much? 43
Grow a name 44
Name badges 45
Bringing the bread 46
Where is it? 47
Fill up the counter 48
What can you clap? 49
Making bread 50
Give a hand 51
Baker's shop 52
We care and share 53
Baking bread 54

Ducks love rain 80
Listen to the weather 81
Stormy weather 82
Noah's ark 83
Ducks and frogs 84
Who built the ark? 85
Pitter patter raindrops 86

chapter four

The wheels on the bus

Introduction 55
I'm on the bus 56
Look out! 57
How many wheels? 58
Circles everywhere 59
Slow down! 60
Who's on the bus? 61
No wheels 62
Where shall we go? 63
Busy street 64
Listen for the bus 65
Bus drivers 66
Signs for safety 67
Our street 68
Round and round 69
Wheels to eat 70

photocopiable activities

Making tea 87
Which teapots match? 88
Label the parts 89
What do you know? 90
How many cakes? 91
Follow the paths 92
Who's on the bus? 93
Match the wheels 94
Match the pairs 95
Which clothes will you wear? 96

chapter five

I hear thunder

Introduction 71
Wellington boots 72
Is that thunder? 73
Running home 74
How many frogs? 75
Float or sink 76
Frogs in a pond 77
Then and now 78
Which season? 79

The golden rule for anyone trying to teach young children is to start with what they know. For this reason using nursery rhymes as the basis for teaching ideas is such a good idea!

Most children starting playgroup or nursery for the first time will have at least a smattering of nursery rhymes at their command. Those who haven't will soon learn them, through constant repetition, by enjoying and practising them with the rest of the group.

Once the children feel secure in their knowledge, and feel that the rhymes 'belong' to them they will be full of confidence and ready to begin new activities or new learning sessions. Their confidence will make them enthusiastic to tackle the new ideas or tasks, because they have a familiar starting point.

Rhymes are so easily and eagerly learned by nature of their repetitive parts and their rhythms, they make the perfect starting point. For this book we have selected the five most well-known and popular 'action' rhymes to provide a range of activities in all areas of the curriculum.

Getting ready for school
The activities in this book are designed for children who are working towards Key Stage 1 and tie in with the National Curriculum for Key Stage 1 and the Scottish National Guidelines 5–14. Each chapter provides: two activities to cover English, two for mathematics and one each for science, design and technology, history, geography, art, music, PE and RE as well as two on display and finally a cookery activity. The activities also link with the *Desirable Outcomes for Children's Learning* for five-year-olds identified by the School Curriculum and Assessment Authority, providing a suitable curriculum for playgroups, pre-school groups and nurseries as well as for children in school reception classes.

Using this book
Each chapter is based on a specific rhyme and obviously this rhyme needs to be learned and practised regularly. It is amazing how quickly small children can 'forget' so always begin each task with a recap of the rhyme.

You can treat each chapter as a 'topic'. The activities within a chapter do not need to be tackled in the specific order in which they are written, but some do follow on from each other. The best approach is to be flexible, picking out a subject area which is most likely to interest the children at any time, or selecting an activity which is most easily resourced at any specific time.

Each activity is laid out in the same format with learning objective, group sizes, details of things you will need and any necessary

preparation listed. The activity itself is then described and useful discussion areas are highlighted. Ways to support younger children and ideas to extend older children are also provided and further ideas for follow-up activities are also given.

Displays

At the end of each chapter, ideas for displaying the work that the children have done are provided. These displays are an important part of the 'topic' since they will reinforce all the children's learning, and should also stimulate plenty of talking and listening. Ideally you could mount the displays with the children having some input – such as helping to decide where to put certain things – so that they all feel that the display does, indeed, 'belong' to them. Obviously, in practice, this may be difficult, so you could put up the display when the children aren't around, and use it as a focal point for the day's work next time the group meets.

Cookery

Establish a regular hygiene routine before any cookery activity, making sure all children wear a protective apron and wash their hands thoroughly. Be sensitive to individual children's cultural or religious customs, and practices such as vegetarianism which will limit the consumption of some foods. Ensure that you are aware of any food allergies, intolerances or special dietary requirements and that all relevant information is documented for other staff.

Using adult helpers

Most of the activities will work best in small groups, if there are extra adult helpers available the children in the whole group could be split into small groups, each with an adult helper, so that they could all working on the same activity at the same time. Bear in mind that if you do this, the children may be at different levels of ability so you will need to observe carefully where children may need extra help or where they are able to work more independently.

With drama and movement activities it would be very helpful to have other adults amongst the children, following the instructions and acting as role models, to encourage the children into imaginative interpretations of the tasks.

Make sure any adult helpers read through and discuss the activities before the sessions begin, so that everybody knows exactly what they are doing.

Links with home

If possible, invite parents in to see the work their children have achieved based on the nursery rhymes. Parents are often amazed to see how much more their children can get out of a rhyme than simply learning to recite it or act it out. Encourage the children to tell their parents about the games and activities they have taken part in – this will not only help to develop their language skills but will also reinforce the learning that has taken place.

chapter one
▶ **introduction** ◀

I'm a Little Teapot

I'm a lit - tle tea - pot, short and stout, Here's my han - dle, here's my spout.

When I see the tea - cups, hear me shout, "Tip me up and pour me out!"

I'm a little teapot, short and stout
Stand with feet a little way apart and arms stretched wide
Here's my handle, here's my spout
*Bend elbow and place one hand on hip for handle; stretch the
other arm to the side, above shoulder height, for the spout*
When I see the teacups, hear me shout
Shrug shoulders on 'shout'
'Tip me up and pour me out!'
Tilt sideways, first towards the bent elbow and then towards the outstretched arm.

Many children may come into play group or nursery knowing this nursery rhyme well, others may have never seen a teapot! Whatever your starting point with the children, the rhyme has lots of potential for activities in maths, English, science and all other areas of the curriculum.

The song has a nice, bouncy rhythm and the movements mimic a squat, rounded traditional teapot.

Demonstrate the actions as you sing the rhyme and let the children copy you. Next encourage them to work through the song and actions only looking to you when they forget the words or what to do. Try getting the children to join in doing the actions of the rhyme without singing the words, which will help them to learn concentration as they'll have to think harder about what they're doing.

Since the invention of the tea-bag lots of people never use teapots! As some children won't have any idea of how tea was originally made in pots, it would be a good idea to show them a teapot and explain how tea was made with loose tea-leaves and left to stand in the pot before it was poured, long before individual tea-bags and mugs were invented! This simple fact is a piece of history for the children.

With a bit of imagination it is possible to use the rhyme as the starting point for a wide variety of activities across the whole early years curriculum.

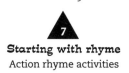

Make a teapot book

Objective
English – to make a shape book giving instructions.

Group size
Four or five children.

What you need
Unbreakable teapot, cups and saucers, mugs, milk jug, sugar bowl, spoons, tea-bags, water, coloured card, sugar paper, scissors, felt-tipped pen, stapler or string.

Preparation
Show the children how to make tea in the pot, using cool water, and how to pour it into the cups, discussing what you are doing, providing all the necessary vocabulary. Encourage the children to play at making and pouring tea for each other.

What to do
Tell them they are going to make, write and illustrate a group book giving instructions for making tea.

With the children watching, draw a large teapot shape on the card and cut it out. Draw round the cut-out and make another one the same. These card cut-outs can be used by the children as templates to draw round on the sugar paper and they will then form the front and back covers of the book. Cut the shapes out of sugar paper for the pages, if the spouts are too floppy, cut them off!

On the first page write: 'Fill the kettle with water and switch it on'. Read the words to the children then ask them what comes next. When they have decided, write these words on the next page. Continue until you have covered all the instructions. If any of the children can copy or trace the words, encourage them to do so. When complete tie or staple the pages and covers together.

Discussion
Work out a title for the book together. Can you read any of the pages? Can you remember what any page says? Can anyone tell me how to make a pot of tea and pour it out? Can you tell it in the right order?

For younger children
Let them illustrate the book by drawing and colouring pictures on white paper. Draw a strong frame round each picture with a coloured felt-tipped pen and cut round the outside of the frame. Help the children to stick their pictures on the pages.

For older children
Help them to make individual books, rather than one group book. Allow them plenty of time for writing, illustrating and reading their work back.

Follow-up activities
▲ Read the book regularly together. Point out specific words, show that the print runs from left to right and encourage the children to describe the pictures.

▲ Make books showing other activities, for example getting ready for bed at night.

▲ Make books in other shapes – try mug-shaped books for number activities, with one mug on the first page, two on the second, three on the third, and so on.

▲ Use photocopiable page 87 to practise sequencing instructions. Be aware of cultural variations in the way that some families may make tea.

Post in the pot

Objective
English – to develop whole-word recognition skills.

Group size
Whole group.

What you need
Large unbreakable teapot, stiff card cut into small rectangles, felt-tipped pen.

Preparation
Ensure that all the children can repeat the words of the nursery rhyme and that they are familiar with words to do with tea, such as, 'mug', 'cup' and 'spoon'.

What to do
Sit the children in a group and show them the teapot; take off its lid. Tell them they are going to choose and learn words from the rhyme or to do with having a cup of tea.

Help the children to choose simple words. Begin with about five such as 'tea', 'cup', 'tip', 'pour' and 'pot'. Print each word on to a small piece of card as it is chosen and hold it up to show the children. Run your finger from left to right along each word so that they know the direction to read it in. Encourage the children to repeat the word after you several times. Build up the number of words according to the children's response.

Mix the cards up, hold one up and ask for a volunteer to tell the group what the word says. Help them by giving the beginning and ending sounds, pointing to the appropriate letters. If the child is right let them take the word from you and post it into the teapot. Continue with the rest of the words.

Discussion
Talk about the sounds that the words begin with. Which words begin with the same sounds? Which words begin with 't', 's', 'p' or 'sh'? Do you know any more words that begin with these sounds?

For younger children
To give all the children a fair chance at identifying words and posting them, print their own names on card too. Help them to recognise and to post their own names.

For older children
Vary the game by placing the cards down on a surface and asking one child at a time to search for a chosen word amongst them, for example, ask: Who can find the word, tea?

Follow-up activities
▲ Add more words to the collection. Keep them short and simple and use words with the same beginning/ending sounds.
▲ Make cards showing different numbers (show numerals and words) of cups, spoons and so on and play the same game to aid number recognition.
▲ Play 'Whose word?' Deal the word cards out, call out a word and tell the child who has it to stand up. When all the children are standing collect the cards and start again.

Mugs and spoons

Objective
Mathematics – to develop counting and one-to-one correspondence.

Group size
Pairs.

What you need
Dolls, teddy bears, animal toys, twelve small pieces of card, felt-tipped pens, scissors.

Preparation
On six cards draw a mug and on the other six draw a spoon. Talk to the children about having a toys' tea-party.

What to do
Give one child all the 'mugs' and the other all the 'spoons'. Sit a number of toys around a 'tea-table' and help the children to count them. The child with the mugs must give one to each toy, counting as she does so. How many has she used? Can she count how many she has left? The child with the spoons then does the same. Have they used the same number of mugs and spoons? Have they the same number left? Change the number of toys round the tea-table and start again.

Discussion
Talk about what would happen if more toys were invited to the tea-party. How could you make sure you had enough mugs and spoons? If you invited three more toys, how many more mugs would you need? How many spoons?

For younger children
Keep the counting sessions short, five or ten minutes a day will help them to gain counting confidence.

For older children
Extend the activity by asking them to work out how many toys could be at the tea-party if each toy had to have two mugs and two spoons? How many toys could they have if they only had to have either a mug or a spoon? When they are confident with six, start again, counting to ten.

Follow-up activities
▲ Make more cards, showing tea-bags and a pot. Invite the children to count different numbers of tea-bags into the pot.
▲ Write the numbers 1 to 10 on pieces of card. Put down a number of picture cards and ask individual children to find the right number.
▲ Teach them a song (to the tune of 'Frère Jacques'): 'Mugs and spoons, mugs and spoons; Teapots too, teapots too; Sugar basin, milk jug, sugar basin, milk jug; Who'd like tea? Who'd like tea?'. Make up other words to fit the tune!

Match the teapots

Objective
Mathematics – to develop shape and colour recognition.

Group size
Four or five children.

What you need
Large sheet of card, felt-tipped pen, scissors, three different coloured crayons, adhesive.

Preparation
The children need to have had some experience of recognising colours and identifying shapes. Cut the card into nine equal pieces. Draw three square-shaped teapots, three round-shaped teapots and three triangular-shaped teapots. Make sure they all have a handle and a spout. Colour the teapots, in order: yellow, blue, yellow, blue, red, red, red, blue, yellow. Leave the teapot lids blank.

What to do
Mix the cards up and place them on a flat surface. Ask the children to take turns. Ask them to find: two teapots that are the same shape; two teapots that are the same colour; two teapots that are the same shape **and** the same colour; two teapots that are **not** the same shape and **not** the same colour.

Discussion
Talk about the properties of shape and colour. What is the same about all the teapots? What is different about them? Count the teapots, how many are there altogether? If you take all the red ones away, how many are left?

For younger children
Encourage them to create a teapot shape of their own; can they make two to match? What colours should they make them? Will they match any of the other teapots in colour?

For older children
Ask them to make up a different pattern for each teapot lid, choose from stripes, spots, squares or circles. They need to create nine different patterns and then fill in the lids when they are sure they have enough for each one to be different.

Follow-up activities
▲ Add three oblong shaped teapots, colour them red, yellow and blue.
▲ Use photocopiable page 88, 'Which teapots match?' to develop shape recognition skills.
▲ Talk about the shapes of the teapots; look for other objects that are round, oblong and triangular.
▲ Make a collection of red things, blue things, yellow things. Label them with the names of the colours.

▲ **11**
Starting with rhyme
Action rhyme activities

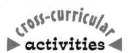

Add some water

Objective
Science – to investigate adding different substances to water.

Group size
Four or five children.

What you need
Water tray, sieves, colanders, slotted spoons, different sized containers, teapot, tea-bag, several small water containers, spoons, food colouring. Substances: sugar, salt, flour, coffee whitener, cocoa, toothpaste, washing-up liquid, jelly cubes.

Preparation
Set up the water tray with the equipment (sieves, colanders) and allow the children to experiment with pouring and tipping.

What to do
When the children are familiar with the different apparatus, ask them if they think they can guess what will happen if they add small amounts of the different substances to the water.

Show them what happens with the tea first. Put the tea-bag in the pot and let one child pour cold water on it, leave it for a few minutes before pouring. The children should be able to guess what has happened to the water.

One-by-one let the children pour a small amount of water into a container and add one spoonful of their chosen substance. Ask them to say what they think will happen. Next tell them to stir it carefully and see what does happen.

Discussion
Talk about what happens. Does it help to stir it in the water? Would it make any difference if the water was warmer? Watch some things disappear in the water (dissolve). Why do some things dissolve and some things not? What happens when we add soap or bubble bath to water?

For younger children
Let the children experiment by just adding washing-up liquid and blowing bubbles. How could they make more lather? What would help them to blow bigger bubbles?

For older children
Try pouring a few drops of food colouring (check for permanency) into the water. What happens? Ask the children to write down what they think will happen and what they actually see from their observations.

Follow-up activities
▲ Experiment with different water temperatures: what happens if the children put one hand in warm water and one in cold, then both in lukewarm?
▲ Encourage the children to bring in from home any pouring apparatus.
▲ Use different materials and soak and squeeze – sponge fabric/clay/wood/polystyrene/stone/paper to see if the water can be squeezed out.

Cups and saucers

Objective
Design and Technology – to make a set of cups and saucers.

Group size
Three or four children.

What you need
Card, yoghurt pots, scissors, PVA adhesive, small coloured sticky paper shapes.

Preparation
Have a card circle ready to use as a template for the saucers. Cut strips of card 5cm x 1cm for the cup handles.

What to do
To make the saucers, help the children to draw and cut round your circle template. Use the yoghurt pots to make the cups. The children need to make a handle to stick on to their pots. To do this glue one end of a card strip near the top of the yoghurt pot, bend the strip back and glue it near the bottom of the pot. They will have to hold the handles on until the glue has dried.

Let the children decorate their cup and saucer with the sticky paper shapes.

Discussion
Talk about the decorations on the cups and saucers. Can you make the saucers match the cups? Can you make your decoration different from everyone else's so that you can recognise your own cup and saucer?

For younger children
Limit the children to two types of shapes, in two different colours.

For older children
Make more cups and saucers but ask the children to follow a specific pattern for decorating them. Give them small pieces of different shaped and coloured sticky paper and give specific instructions such as: 'Stick three yellow stars at the top of the cup; stick a blue square underneath the first yellow star'.

Follow-up activities
▲ Have a tea party, pouring the 'tea' into their cups.
▲ Place a random selection of the cups and saucers on a tray, let the children look at it for a few seconds, then cover it with a cloth. Who can remember what was on the tray? Add or take some away, show the children for a few seconds before covering the tray. What's on the tray this time?

Starting with rhyme
Action rhyme activities

This is the way

Objective
History – drama work to show the sequence of events from planting to drinking tea.

Group size
Whole group.

What you need
Lots of space, tea-leaves, tea-bags.

Preparation
Bring in some loose tea-leaves and some tea-bags to show the children. Tell them that tea grows in countries far away, as a shrub or a bush. Explain that the tea-leaves are picked and dried before being prepared and sold all over the world. Explain that when the tea arrives at our homes it has already been through many processes and this has taken a lot of time from when it was first sown as a seed.

What to do
The children need space to act out the story of tea. Talk them through it as they do the actions. First they need to be tea-workers, digging at the soil and carefully planting the seedlings. Water the plants to help them grow. When the leaves are ready, pick them from the bushes, stretching high up to get the best leaves. Lay them flat to dry. When they are dry they are loaded onto trucks and then ships.

The next step is to act out buying tea in the supermarket. Then to take it home and put the kettle on. Get out their teapot and a cup, saucer, spoon and milk from a cupboard. Put the tea-bag into the teapot, switch off the kettle and carefully pour on the hot water. Put milk in the cup, pour out the tea, stir it and drink it.

Discussion
Talk through the sequence of events with the children. What was the first thing that happened? What was the last thing? What happened after the tea-leaves were picked? What happened before the leaves were packed? How did the leaves get here? How long do you think it took to grow the tea, dry it and send it abroad?

For younger children
Encourage them to remember and verbalise, or act out, as much of the sequence as they can. Invite them to draw two pictures, in order of what happens.

For older children
Talk about the countries where tea grows: Japan, China, Sri Lanka and India. Point out the countries on a map and show the children how far away they are.

Follow-up activities
▲ Go through any sequences of events the children can tell you about, such as getting up and going to bed.
▲ Practise saying the sequence of days in a week; months in a year.
▲ Make a chart of the children's birthday months and display it for them to refer to.

Place the teapot

Objective
Geography – to reinforce the concept of space and place.

Group size
Whole group.

What you need
Unbreakable teapot.

Preparation
Talk about where things are – what town do the children live in, which street are they in, what kind of building are they in, what room are they in?

What to do
Begin the game by placing the teapot on a surface and asking the children, 'Where is the teapot?'. They should be able to reply 'On the table'. The next question is 'Where is the table?' and the answer should be 'In the room'. Ask 'Where is the room?'.

At every reply, you ask where the place is that they answer, encouraging the children to extend their ideas of 'space' and 'place' until they reach the furthest spot possible.

Discussion
Put the teapot in different places and see how differently the questions can be answered. For example if you are working outside, place the teapot on a garden bench or in a tree. The beginning of the game may always be different but the children should eventually get to the same points.

For younger children
Play 'Where is it?' games – encouraging the children to use positional language, such as 'on' 'under' 'across from' 'opposite' 'against' 'in front of' 'behind'.

For older children
Ask them to draw a picture beginning with the teapot on the table in the centre and gradually working out to show the whole situation of the teapot in its own position in the universe.

Follow-up activities
▲ Draw a simple map of your location, showing the community around where you are. Can the children tell you their route to your group and then follow it together on the map?

▲ Ask the children to draw pictures of themselves at home showing another place (shops/park/school), in relation to their home.

▲ Make up a song (to the tune of 'Here we go round the mulberry bush'): 'Here we go down the corridor; Here we go over the road to the shops; Here we go through the shopping centre' and so on.

▲ 15
Starting with rhyme
Action rhyme activities

Pretty pot patterns

Objective
Art – to create patterns using different colours and shapes.

Group size
Three to five children.

What you need
Card, scissors, scraps of coloured fabric, scraps of coloured paper, adhesive, crayons.

Preparation
Draw a large teapot shape on card, cut it out and use as a template to provide each child with a teapot shape.

What to do
Talk about patterns together and show the children how to do stripes, spots, checks and other patterns using crayons on the plain paper. Encourage them to develop the idea of repeating one or two shapes to make a pattern.

Tell the children to each select two patterns for their teapot, one to draw on each side. Help them to cut out paper and fabric to make the patterns and glue them to each side of the teapots.

Discussion
Explain that patterns are all around us. Ask the children to tell you what their favourite patterns are. Can you describe them in words? Where can you find them? Why do you like them? Which patterns do you have on your clothes? What are your favourite colours for patterns?

For younger children
Encourage the children to look for patterns on their clothing or around the room; can they copy them with crayons or by cutting and sticking?

For older children
Talk about how patterns can change if they use different colours. What would happen if they used more colours? Could they do the same pattern but using four colours instead of two? How would they decide when to repeat each colour?

Follow-up activities
▲ Go for a 'Pattern walk' – take paper and pencils and draw interesting patterns (found on buildings, the pavement, on flowers or leaves). Stick the pictures into a scrapbook to make a 'Pattern Book'.
▲ Point out patterns that can be found on the building and on clothing.
▲ Words have patterns too – listen to nursery rhymes on tape and help the children to find rhyming words and words that have the same beginning or ending sounds.

Sounds like

Objective
Music – to make 'watery' percussion sounds.

Group size
Three or four children.

What you need
Some of the following percussion instruments: tambourine, handbells, wooden blocks, rhythm sticks, shakers. Washing-up liquid bottle with peas, spoons and boxes, milk bottle tops, string or wool.

Preparation
Collect any percussion instruments that you can find. If you do not have real instruments you can use home-made ones. You need things to shake and things to bang. To make a shaker, thread milk bottle tops on to string or wool. For bangers use cardboard boxes with wooden spoons. Try and find as many different sounds as possible.

What to do
Ask the children to think how many different sounds water makes. You will have to help them with the vocabulary but encourage them to say words like 'drip' or 'trickle'.

Let the children practise making the sounds they have thought of with their mouths and hands, then invite them to use the percussion instruments to make sounds appropriate to the words. For example, 'drip' might be a slow, light beat on the drum.

Discussion
Talk about how the words themselves make sounds. Sing, 'Let's all clap together' but use the water words instead of the actions, singing, 'Let's all splosh together' and make big 'splosh, splosh splosh' sounds for the next bit of the song.

For younger children
When the children are familiar with the vocabulary, ask them to find a space and to move to the sound of the words. For example, 'splosh' might be a quick little jump from two feet to two feet.

For older children
Play a guessing game where each child in turn chooses a word and makes a percussion sound or a movement which represents it, see if the other children in the group can guess which word it is.

Follow-up activities
▲ Learn a 'watery' song, (to the tune of 'She'll be coming round the mountains'): 'Oh, we're splashing in the water in the bath/Oh we're sloshing in a puddle in our boots/Oh we're trickling like a raindrop on the pane/Oh we're gushing like a river down the drain' and so on, and do some actions to match the words.

▲ Use the percussion instruments for counting practice by teaching the children how to count one, two, three, for a space between turns. For example, ask for two 'splosh' sounds and a space of three, then two trickle sounds and a space of three and so on.

▲ Make a book of water words and pictures.

Pottery shapes

Objective
PE – to make different body shapes, to listen to commands and interpret them.

Group size
Whole group.

What you need
Plenty of space to move in.

Preparation
Make sure the children understand words like *long*, *round*, *fat*, *thin*, *twisting*, *handle*, *spout*. It will help if they are familiar with the game 'Simon Says'.

What to do
Ask the children to each find a space where they can swing their arms around wide enough not to hit anybody else.

Explain how to play the game: the leader calls out 'pottery shapes can be round' and all the children must make themselves round. The leader calls out 'pottery shapes can be as thin as a pin' and all the children must try to make themselves thin. The leader may say 'pottery shapes can lean to the left' and the children do so. But if the leader says, 'they have handles', without using the magic words 'pottery shapes', then any child that makes the movement is 'out'.

Discussion
Talk about the different shapes and movements that the children can make by moving their bodies. Ask them to suggest some new words that you can incorporate into the game – twisty, pointed, curvy, wobbly, straight or frozen for example. Ask them if they know of any other 'magic words'.

For younger children
Start with the children sitting in one space, they can then easily make shapes and move their arms and legs without bumping into anyone else, until they really understand the game.

For older children
Try to speed up their interpretation and responses by giving the instructions faster and find ways of introducing new movement words, such as 'leap', 'squat', 'rock'.

Follow-up activities
▲ Use the game to give other instructions such as: pottery shapes get into a line; pottery shapes walk round in a circle; pottery shapes all sit down.
▲ Look for shapes around you; reinforce the idea of 'square', 'triangle', 'circle', 'oblong', whenever you can.
▲ Play 'Follow My Leader' with the first child in the line deciding on a shape and way of moving and the rest of the children imitating. The leader goes to the back of the line and the second child has a go.

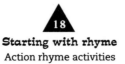

Invite a friend

Objective
RE – to organise a tea-party.

Group size
Whole group for organising the party; small groups for making the invitations.

What you need
Card, coloured pencils or crayons, scissors, food and drink for tea-party (see page 22).

Preparation
Cut the card into A5 pieces for an invitation. Draw a line for the child's name, and write 'Invites' then draw a line for the name of the child who will receive the card. Write 'To a tea-party'.

What to do
Talk to the children about having a tea-party. Try and emphasise the importance of sharing social occasions, of having fun together and behaving well. Ask: if they were having a tea-party who would they invite? What would they have to eat? What games could they play?

Help the children to organise a real tea-party that you can have together one morning or afternoon. Explain that they don't have to drink tea, they can drink squash but pour it from a teapot!

Hand out the A5 cards and help them to write their own names in the first space, and someone else's name in the second space. Make sure that every child both sends and receives an invitation. Work with the children in small groups to make invitations for each other.

Discussion
Encourage the children to tell the group about invitations they have sent out or received before. What kind of information was on your invitations? What did the replies say? Do you think we have got all the information we need?

For younger children
Pin the invitations up on a wall and encourage the children to look for their own names. Help them to begin to recognise the names of friends.

For older children
Ask the children if they can think of any other information they might need on the invitations, perhaps they could write the day and time. Let them decorate their invitations with teapots and teacups.

Follow-up activities
▲ Make the baby pizzas from page 22 to have at the party.
▲ Have the tea-party, make it a happy social occasion for all the children.
▲ Collect old birthday cards, let the children choose pictures to cut out and stick to their invitations.
▲ Make invitations to parents to come in and see the work the group has been doing.

Come to our tea-party!

What you need
Card, scissors, felt-tipped pen, reel of cotton, sticky tape, Copydex glue, table, cloth, toy tea-set/s, kettle, tea-bags, empty milk carton, sugar in bowl.

Preparation
Collect together all the art work which the children have done, including the decorated teapots from 'Pretty pot patterns' on page 16, the invitations to the tea-party on page 19 and the cup and saucers from page 13. Print the words the children learned in 'Sounds like' page 17, large on coloured card cut into the shape of mugs or teapots.

What to do
If possible cover a wall with either wallpaper or frieze paper and then arrange the children's invitations and the cups and saucers on the wall affixing them with rolled up sticky tape, or Copydex.

Thread different lengths of cotton through the top of the teapots and hang them at random points all over the display.

Hang some in front of the display, suspended from a piece of string if possible.

Place a table in front of the wall display, cover it with the cloth and arrange the toy tea-set on it making sure there is a cup for each saucer and a spoon for each cup. Put the kettle, tea-bags, empty milk carton and sugar bowl towards the back of the table where they won't be handled. Prop up the teapot-shaped book on display.

Give your display a large heading such as 'Come to our tea-party'. Print the words of the rhyme on a large piece of card and fasten it to the wall.

Discussion
Ask the children where are the teapots/cups/saucers? They must answer with a description, not point and say 'There'. Who can talk through the sequence for making tea from the table display? Can you remember how the tea grew? Where did it come from? How did it get to the shop? Who can read a word from the wall? How many cups and saucers are there?

I'm a little teapot, short and stout,
Here's my handle, here's my spout
When I see the tea-cups, hear me shout,
"Tip me up and pour me out!"

Our teapot book

milk

How many?

What you need
Card, scissors, felt-tipped pen, pictures of teapots, cups and saucers, picture of baby pizzas, words from 'Post in the pot' page 9.

Preparation
Collect together some of the children's pieces of work including some of the cut-out cups and saucers, some of the card teapots and some pictures of the baby pizzas. Draw ten spoons on card and cut them out.

What to do
Cover the wall with wallpaper or frieze paper. Arrange a set of pictures of cups and saucers, stick them to the wall. Write a label, 'How many cups and saucers can you see?'. Arrange some teapots and stick them up too, write 'How many teapots are here?'. Arrange the pictures of two or three baby pizzas. Write 'We are having baby pizzas for our tea-party'. Cut two more baby pizzas in half. Write 'How many children can have pizza?'.

Arrange a line of card spoons along the bottom of the display and write 'Count the spoons.' Arrange another line of words from the 'Post in the pot' game. Write 'Do you know these words?'.

Discussion
Ask the children to remember how the baby pizzas were made. Ask more open-ended questions – who likes baby pizzas? Why do you like them? Do you have pizzas at home? What is your favourite kind of pizza? Can you count the spoons? Can you put the same number of spoons on the table in front of you? Can you put the number of spoons which is one less than the ones on the wall/ two more than the ones on the wall? (Vary the numbers.) Can you read the words on the wall? Who can find the same words in the teapot book? Can you find words on cards to match? Can you think of more words we could put on the wall? Can you find any of the words in the nursery rhyme?

▲ 21
Starting with rhyme
Action rhyme activities

Baby pizzas

Group size
Three or four children.

What you need
Grill or oven, muffins, jar of tomato pizza topping, grated cheese. Tomato, cucumber, peppers (optional).

Preparation
Make sure everyone washes their hands carefully. Slice the muffins in half, grate the cheese. Heat up the grill and lightly toast the cut sides of the muffins, or put them in a hot oven for about a minute.

What to do
Help the children to sprinkle grated cheese on the toasted side of each muffin. Put them back under the grill or in the oven until the cheese begins to melt. Take them out and spoon a little tomato topping over the cheese and then let the children sprinkle more grated cheese on top. Grill or bake until all the cheese has melted.

The cheese will be very hot so make sure the children understand they cannot touch until it cools down. Cut each baby pizza into halves or quarters for the tea-party.

If the children want to, let them decorate their pizzas with slices of tomatoes, cucumber, red and yellow pepper (be sure

to discard the seeds). Before you begin, help the children to work out how many baby pizzas you will need for the tea-party, and how many muffins you need to use if each muffin makes two baby pizzas.

Discussion
Talk about safety when cooking. Make sure everyone understands that they must not touch hot things. Ask them why it's important to wash their hands carefully before beginning to handle food. How do the pizzas change when they get hot? What happens to the cheese? How many slices can you cut the pizzas into? Can we cut them in halves? Quarters?

Follow-up activities
▲ Can the children remember how they made the baby pizzas? Give each child a sheet of paper divided into four boxes. In the first box write: *We had*; in the second box write: *This is what we did first*; in the third box write: *Next, we...* and in the last box write: *These are the baby pizzas*. Fill in the boxes with illustrations of what happened.
▲ Invite the children to verbalise the activity in sequence.
▲ Make up a pizza memory game. You start with 'On my pizza I had cheese', the next person adds something, and so on.

Here We Go Round the Mulberry Bush

1. Here we go round the mul-ber-ry bush, The mul-ber-ry bush, The mul-ber-ry bush.

Here we go round the mul-ber-ry bush, On a cold and frost-y morn - ing.

This nursery rhyme is especially useful with small children because it lends itself to so many variations; with a little imagination you can easily fit words to the tune to enhance any area of the curriculum.

To begin with, the children need to learn how to walk or skip round in a circle, holding hands. To this action they sing the chorus:

'Here we go round the mulberry bush, the mulberry bush, the mulberry bush. Here we go round the mulberry bush, on a cold and frosty morning'.

The circle now stops and the children loose hands. Add verses: 'This is the way we clap our hands, clap our hands, clap our hands, This is the way we clap our hands on a cold and frosty morning'. Add others: 'This is the way we nod our heads/ stamp our feet...'.

Very young children will enjoy responding with the appropriate action as you sing the words and introduce new movements. As they get older you can add more complicated patterns of movement. You might go through the actions of a whole day: 'This is the way we jump out of bed... wash our face... brush our hair... clean our teeth... go to school' and so on, ending with going back to bed.

Eventually the children will be able to suggest actions and tasks themselves for the rhyme. Use their suggestions to develop social skills and simple control exercises such as following the leader, moving and stopping, becoming still and quiet, tiptoeing back to your room.

The activities in this chapter provide opportunities to explore all kinds of ideas with the children. You will find that this action rhyme improves with repetition and that the children will love to repeat their favourite activities. Use the control exercises to nip over-excitement in the bud and don't hesitate to use your voice also. You have only to sing: 'This is the way we're calm and hushed...' in a whispering voice for all the children to quieten down and copy you with immediate effect!

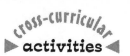
Whether the weather

Objective
English – to dramatise the language of the rhyme.

Group size
Whole group.

What you need
Lots of space.

Preparation
Ensure that the children can repeat the words of the rhyme and understand the concepts of 'cold' and 'frosty'. Discuss what a 'cold and frosty morning' is like. How would they dress? How would they feel?

What to do
Sit the children in a circle and tell them you are going to make up a short play about a cold and frosty morning. Encourage them to suggest words that are connected with cold and frost, for example 'shiver', 'icy', 'icicle', 'freeze', 'chilly'. Use the words they have contributed regularly in your narration.

As you narrate the story the children can act it out. Tell them to start by lying down as if asleep in their warm beds. The alarm goes and it's time for them to wake. They start to climb out of their beds and it's so cold and frosty that they cover themselves back up again. But they have to get out. They sit at the edge of the bed, shivering and trembling with cold. They put on warm clothes and hug themselves to keep out the frost.

Outside on the window, icicles hang. The children freeze into icicle shapes. They become Jack Frost who has to paint all the houses and trees white. The children make spiky, jerking movements and icy, jagged shapes, as they explore the space, painting the houses and trees.

Discussion
What does it feel like to be an icicle? Have you seen ice and frost patterns on windows? Which words felt the coldest? Do you know any more 'cold' words?

For younger children
Ask the children to describe in words how they think Jack Frost moves.

For older children
Continue the story with the children building a snowman. Let the children dance as snowmen and ask them to describe the snowman's movements.

Follow-up activities
▲ Ask the children to draw a cold and frosty morning picture, and write 'cold and frosty' on it.
▲ Play a game of icy statues with the children moving on tip-toe and suddenly freezing into a shape when you call 'freeze!' or 'icicle!'. Let the children choose to be icicles, Jack Frost or the snowmen and to slowly melt each part of their body until they are small shapes on the ground.

Starting with rhyme
Action rhyme activities

Jack Frost

Objective
English – to write a group poem, following discussion.

Group size
Five or six children.

What you need
Paper, pencils, crayons, card.

Preparation
Talk about the concepts of cold, frost and Jack Frost. Ideally, carry out the previous drama activity 'Whether the weather' on page 24 before you begin. Tell the children that Jack Frost isn't 'real' but that storybooks tell us he comes round to 'paint' everything white and frosty on cold nights.

What to do
Give the children a chorus for the poem. This might be:
'Jack Frost comes out when it's cold at night/ To paint our trees and houses white'.

Tell them that you are going to make up the rest of the poem together. Explain that it doesn't have to rhyme and that you need to make up about three or four lines in between each chorus.

Talk about what it's like when Jack Frost is about. Is it night-time? Is it dark? Is it cold? Get the children to make up a line for the poem from this discussion.

Discuss how Jack Frost paints the frosty scenes. Does he use his fingers? What are they like? What kind of movements does he make? Again, write a line for the poem.

Where does Jack Frost paint? In the fields? In the streets? On the window panes? Write a line for the poem.

How do you know Jack Frost has been about? Are the roads and pavements frosty? The leaves? How cold is it? Write a line for the poem.

Copy the poem out on to a poster-sized piece of card and help the children to read and learn it.

Discussion
Can you think of other things for Jack Frost to do in the poem? Could he dance or sing? Think of more 'cold' and 'frosty' words that can go into the poem.

For younger children
Help the children to learn the poem off by heart and recite it with you. Until they have learned it all, let them join in with the chorus, which will help them to listen for their turn.

For older children
The children can copy the words out and illustrate their own copy. Encourage them to think up additional lines of their own.

Follow-up activities
▲ Write poems for other weather conditions with a chorus of: 'On a bright and sunny day/When we all come out to play...' .
▲ Make flashcards of the key words and use them for sorting and picking out the right words.
▲ Ask the children to think of more words that begin with 'fr' or end with 'st'.

Look at leaves

Objective
Mathematics – to sort and match different shapes and sizes.

Group size
Up to six children.

What you need
An information book to show leaves, trees and shrubs, small pieces of card, felt-tipped pens.

Preparation
Copy pictures of different sized and differently shaped leaves from the information book, to provide six pictures of each leaf. Talk about the fact that plants, bushes and trees have leaves, and that each plant's leaves are different. Have a collection of twigs, branches and flowers with leaves on a nature table and point out the differences in the leaves to the children.

What to do
Spread all the leaf cards out on a table or desk and ask the children to sort them into sets. Ask each child to take a different leaf and to find all the other leaves that are the same to make a set. Ask the children, how many sets of leaves there are all together.

Once the sets have been sorted, mix all the cards up again. Ask the children to each find a set of six leaves which are all different.

Again, mix the leaf cards and ask the children to sort all the leaves into pairs. How many sets of pairs can they make?

Mix the cards up for a final time and get the children to sort them into sets going from the smallest leaf to the largest.

Discussion
Talk about what is the same about the leaves and what is different. Are they all the same size? Are they all the same colour? Do they all have the same pattern? Do they all have the same shape? What is different about the shapes?

For younger children
Invite the children to trace over the leaves and colour them in. They can stick their tracings into a book and label them: small, smaller, smallest and big, bigger, biggest.

For older children
Help the children to make a 'leaf book'. Copy the shape of a leaf, cut it out three or four times to make the pages. Help them to make up leaf picture sums on the pages.

Follow-up activities
▲ Place all the cards face down on the table and play 'Pairs', the children take turns to turn over two cards at a time and keep any pairs they find. The winner is the child with the most pairs at the end.
▲ Collect some leaves, stand them in a container of water and wait to see if roots form. If they do, plant them – they will grow into new plants.
▲ Use the leaf cards to play adding and subtracting games.

▲ 26
Starting with rhyme
Action rhyme activities

How many berries?

Objective
Mathematics – to become familiar with numbers up to nine.

Group size
Pairs.

What you need
Two large sheets of paper, set of plastic numbers, red card, black felt-tipped pen, scissors.

Preparation
Draw two mulberry bushes on the large sheets of paper. Draw 15 spaces for berries and write numbers up to nine on them (use doubles of the number which your children need reinforcing most!). Using the red card, draw and cut out large 'berries'. Put the plastic numbers into a bag.

What to do
Each player has one mulberry bush with 15 berries on. The children take it in turns to pull a plastic number from the bag. If the number matches a number on a berry space they can put a 'berry' on the space. Place the number back in the bag, shake it and the next player has a turn. The first player to cover all the berry spaces on their bush is the winner.

Discussion
Talk about numbers as they apply to the children. How many days do they come to school? How many heads have they got? How many hands? How many fingers? How many knees? How many toes? How many hairs on their heads?

For younger children
Make the bushes smaller and put only eight berry spaces on them. Place numbers up to five in the bag.

For older children
Use numbers up to 20. This will mean making much bigger bushes, with 25 spaces on each, they will need to keep a plastic '1' out of the bag to make up tens and unit numbers.

Follow-up activities
▲ Give each child a sheet of paper with four numbers (up to nine) written on it well spaced-out. Players must look around outside (supervised) and collect objects to match the numbers on their sheets (such as pebbles, twigs, leaves).
▲ Play a number-spotting game. Ask the children to spot two books, three pencils, four boys and so on.

Starting with rhyme
Action rhyme activities

Can you do this?

Objective
Science – to name different body parts.

Group size
Whole group.

What you need
Lots of space.

Preparation
Ensure the children know the words of the rhyme and can sing at least the chorus. Go through naming the parts of the body which you want them to learn.

What to do
Group the children in a circle to sing the chorus and dance or skip in a ring. On the 'This is the way...' part of the song, devise things to do which they copy, which will give them the names of different body parts.

For example: This is the way...
we clean our teeth
we brush our hair
we hang our heads
we touch our necks
we wiggle our ears
we stick out our tongues
we shrug our shoulders
we wave our hands
we fold our arms
we twist our wrists
we tap our elbows
we pat our knees
we point our toes
we stand on our heels
we hold our ankles.

Discussion
Get the children to use the words they find the most difficult. Can you make up something to do with your ankles? Elbows? Shoulders? Wrists? Can you think of something different to do with your knees? Toes? Tongues?

For younger children
Concentrate on the easiest words first. They will find it quite difficult to absorb the concepts of ankles, wrists, shoulders and elbows and you need to reinforce them quite often before they understand them.

For older children
Encourage them to learn the names of even more parts – for instance knuckle, spine, waist, trunk, forehead and eyebrows. Can they think of funny actions to do to help them remember the words?

Follow-up activities
▲ Ask the children to imagine that they are different people (a builder/a fireman/a policeman) and to sing and act out these characters: 'This is the way we dig and paint/climb and lift/stride and plod'.
▲ Use the photocopiable page 89 to reinforce the learning of body parts.
▲ Try adding names to the rhyme and let the child whose name you sing lead the activity – 'This is the way Rashid taps his elbows' and so on.

Sew-a-bush

Objective
Design and Technology – to make a picture using needle and thread.

Group size
Two or three children.

What you need
Card, scissors, felt-tipped pen, size 20 tapestry needles, brightly coloured thread.

Preparation
Cut the card into approximately postcard sizes. Draw a simple bush shape on each card, keeping as close to the edges as you can. Use a thin nail or a tapestry needle to make holes about every centimetre around the edge of the shape.

What to do
Help the children to thread their tapestry needles with brightly coloured thread. Show them how to push the needles through the front and back up through the back, following the line all the way round the bush. You may have to hold the end of the thread at the back to make sure they don't pull it straight through!

When complete, fasten the two ends of the thread off on the back of the card with sticky tape.

Discussion
Encourage them to experiment – what do you think will happen if you pull the string too hard? What will happen if you go into the same hole twice?

For younger children
This will give lots of practice using certain vocabulary – *front* and *back*, *up*, *down* and *through*, as well as *needle, thread, sew*.

For older children
Make the shapes a bit more complicated by drawing in twigs so that the picture needs more holes. Use green thread for the bush and brown thread for the branches and twigs.

Follow-up activities
▲ Draw some more simple shapes to sew; try not to have holes near the centre of the card as it's harder for little fingers to stretch and sew near the middle. Colour in the resulting sewn pictures.
▲ Make some patterns and number the holes. Let the children follow the numbers with their needles.
▲ Draw the shapes of the children's initials for them to sew along.

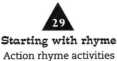

What if...?

Objective
History – to speculate how people lived in past times.

Group size
Whole group.

What you need
Lots of space.

Preparation
Discuss how people lived in the past. Tell the children how water was pumped from wells, food was cooked on fires, people dressed in shawls and sacking material. Make sure all the children can sing the chorus of the rhyme.

What to do
Tell the children they are going to act out a story of life for children in the past. All the children skip in the circle, singing the chorus. On the 'This is the way...' part of the song, give them activities such as:

we pump the water
big pumping action
we splash our faces
splashing water from the pump
we put on our sacking
pulling over head, pushing arms through holes
we tie our aprons
tie sacking round waist
we pull on our shawls
tie shawls round shoulders
we walk in our clogs
clumping in wooden clogs
we light our fires
build up sticks, light by 'passing round' spill
we cook our meat
hang meat over fire
we bake our bread
knead and pat into shape.

Discussion
Talk about what is different about our life and the life of people long ago in the past. Do you think life was harder then? What do you think are the best things we have today that they didn't have then? Why? What would you most hate to do without?

For younger children
Keep the activities as simple as possible and use them as a follow-my-leader game. Once the children are familiar with the activities, let one child choose and lead, with all the others following.

For older children
Help them to understand that things we take for granted like televisions, cars, going to school, having holidays, weren't part of life only a hundred years ago. What would they do with their time if they didn't have TVs? How would they get from one place to another if they didn't have cars, buses, trains and aeroplanes?

Follow-up activities
▲ Invite the children to talk, write and draw about the drama activities they have been doing.
▲ Encourage the children to talk to their grandparents and great-grandparents about how life has changed since they were children. What was different? How do they think their life has improved or worsened?
▲ Make books with double-page spreads. Head the right hand pages 'Then' and the left hand pages 'Now'. Do sections on homes, transport, school, toys and games.

Bush, tree, hedge

Objective
Geography – to explore the environment and different forms of plant life.

Group size
Up to five.

What you need
Outside space, pencils, paper, pictures of bushes, trees and shrubs.

Preparation
When the children sing the rhyme, stop them and ask what a 'bush' is. Discuss the differences between bushes, trees, and smaller plants or flowers, and show them pictures of the three. Play a game identifying which is which.

What to do
Go on a plant walk. Take pencils and paper with you and look for all forms of plant life, help the children to identify whether they are bushes, trees or smaller plants. Find a tree, a bush and a small plant or clump of flowers for the children to draw.

Back inside, help the children to label their drawings. Talk about *where* they found the tree, bush, flowers. Invite them to tell you and the rest of the group the route which they took.

Discussion
Talk about where they might find other bushes, trees, flowers. Do you have any bushes in your garden? Or any trees? How can you recognise a bush? Why do you think people grow bushes in their gardens? Can you describe the differences between trees and bushes? What's the same about them? What's different?

For younger children
Let them decide on the route before you go, with the understanding that you are looking for a way that will show you as much plant life as possible. Let them describe the way, and then check as you go how much plant life you pass.

For older children
Talk about the route when you get back. Ask them to recall any geographical features they can, for example a hill, a road to be crossed, a bridge, a corner to go round, what types of buildings they passed.

Follow-up activities
▲ Invite the children to draw simple maps of the immediate outside environment, drawing on any plant life.
▲ Invite the children to describe the route of their plant walk and what they found, using the terms *up, down, on, under, in front of, behind, near, far, left, right*.
▲ Use the photocopiable page 90 to label features of a map or route and to develop the children's geographical vocabulary.

Forest picture

Objective
Art – to do some weaving, using natural materials.

Group size
Up to six children.

What you need
Stiff card, wool, collection of twigs, leaves and feathers.

Preparation
To make the weaving cards cut v-shapes at the top and bottom of each card. Thread wool over and around the card through the v's, tying the wool at the back to secure it. Collect lots of different twigs, bits of bark, leaves, feathers and any other materials that will be fairly flexible.

What to do
Show the children how to weave over and under with a piece of string or wool.

Give each child a small selection of the natural materials and help them to weave these pieces over and under on their card, remembering that if the first line begins 'over', the second should begin 'under'. Continue until the card is full.

Discussion
Ask the children to think of different kinds of materials they might weave with. Could you use paper? Strips of card? Fabric? What else?

For younger children
Sing the mulberry bush song with them and on 'This is the way ...' sing: 'we weave our leaves/twigs/feathers' and so on, to help build up their vocabulary.

For older children
Show them how to push the pieces they are weaving close together so that there are no gaps. Help them to make choices about the order of the materials they are using.

Follow-up activities
▲ Do weaving in different ways. Use card but instead of threading wool round it cut vertical slits about 4cm apart. Cut strips of card and paper the same width from old magazines and let the children weave a pattern with them.
▲ Change the patterns by cutting diagonal lines instead of vertical lines.

▲ Show the children how to plait (which is a kind of weaving) with three strips of ribbon. Use the plaited lengths to decorate small containers such as yoghurt pots by winding them round and gluing them.
▲ Do a 'feely' piece of weaving, using different textured materials.
▲ Look at some pieces of fabric – can you see any weaving patterns?

Weather sounds

Objective
Music – to make imaginative sounds without instruments.

Group size
Whole group.

What you need
Lots of space.

Preparation
Go through various noises that the children can make with their body, for example whistling, blowing, clapping, stamping. Show them how to click their fingers and invite them to make different sounds with their mouths such as *whoosh, boom, wheeee!*

What to do
Get the children used to the space first by singing two or three choruses of 'Here we go round the mulberry bush' in a circle and then ask them to find a space by themselves.

In their space each child is going to pretend to be a mulberry bush. As you tell the story, the children should decide, together, on noises which might be appropriate, and practise them.

Tell the story of the bush: when the wind is strong it whirls through the bush with a (make a sound such as *whoosh*). The leaves are flung from the bush and twirl up into the air (*swoosh*). They float round and round (sound) before they twirl to the ground (sound). The thunder comes, cracking and rolling across the sky (sound). Lightning flashes (sound). Then it begins to rain, lightly at first (sound), then harder and harder (sound) until the bush is soaking wet. The rain stops but the leaves drip (sound).

Discussion
Talk about different weather sounds. How many different noises can you think of for wind? For rain? For thunder and lightning? What sounds might the mulberry bush make if it's a sunny day? What creatures might hide in the mulberry bush? What sounds would they make? What happens to sounds when there's snow on the ground?

For younger children
Help them to find appropriate sounds for the different parts of the story. They will probably all copy each other but encourage imaginative and creative ideas. If one child has an idea let everybody try it out and decide whether it works.

For older children
After telling them the story let them get together in small groups of three or four and work out a sequence for their sounds. Let them practise and perform their ideas to the class.

Follow-up activities
▲ Change the story, or at least its sequence, and let the children listen and respond in their own movement and sound ways.
▲ Write a poem together using the words of your story and the sounds the children have made. Recite the poem together, putting in the sounds.
▲ Help the children to think of all the onomatopoeic sounds and words that they know. Try and think of some new ones.

How shall we go?

Objective
PE – to explore different ways of travelling.

Group size
Whole group.

What you need
Lots of space.

Preparation
Ensure the children know the words of the rhyme and understand that the activity parts can be changed.

What to do
Have the children in a circle to sing the chorus and dance or skip in a ring. On the 'This is the way...' part of the song, devise things to do which they copy, which will give them different ways to move.

For example: This is the way...
we bounce up and down
we walk on tiptoe
we skip round and round
we stretch and grow
we shrink and curl up
we jump on two feet
we hop along
we leap up high
we spin around
we stamp along
we gallop away
we march to the tune
we trot like a horse
we shake our bodies
we slither like snakes
we creep in the dark.

Discussion
Talk about the actions the children can do. Can you think of any more? Can you make a pattern of three of the movements?

For younger children
Sing the chorus in the circle and then show them each movement you want them to do and give them the words clearly, before they do them.

For older children
Give individuals the chance to suggest a movement, describe it in words, and then demonstrate it before the rest of the group join in.

Follow-up activities
▲ Make up a story to go with the movements. For instance, a story about a giant, stretching on waking, taking huge giant footsteps, creeping in the dark.
▲ Experiment with working on different levels and with moving at different speeds.
▲ Use percussion instruments to get movement response from the children.

Good to know

Objective
RE – to develop good personal attitudes.

Group size
Whole group.

What you need
Lots of space.

Preparation
Make sure the children are familiar with the rhyme. Talk about the kinds of things you can do to help each other, how you can show other people that you are 'good to know'.

What to do
First do the rhyme and its actions in a way the children are familiar with. Suggest that on the 'This is the way...' part of the song you change the words and actions to things that show you are all 'good to know'. Ask the children for suggestions. Some examples to get them started might be:
we smile all day
we help someone who's hurt
we give someone a hug
we make good friends
we share our toys
we take our turn
we hold someone's hand
we dry someone's tears
we keep our things tidy
we show that we care.

The children may need to work out some of the actions more carefully so give the children time to talk and explain just how they would demonstrate their action – it's the talking and listening and joining in that's important to help form good attitudes. Keep the activities positive.

Discussion
Talk about the kinds of ways the children can be nice to other people. Can you think of other ways to show kindness and caring? Do you always remember to be good to know? How should/could you react to someone who isn't always good to know?

For younger children
Encourage them to tell anecdotes about when someone else was 'good to know' to them, as well as to tell about when they have helped someone else.

For older children
Ask them to tell about other people who have been helpful to them, and make up actions and words for those situations.

Follow-up activities
▲ Ask the children to draw a picture of themselves helping someone. Put all the pictures together to make a frieze to display around your room. Label it with words and actions from the rhyme.
▲ Give rewards, such as star points, for anyone helping someone in class.
▲ Have a 'How has someone been good to you?' session regularly once a week. Invite the children to tell anecdotes of when someone has helped them or made them feel good to know.
▲ Encourage the children to share and take turns in an effort to be 'good to know'.

Cold and frosty morning

What you need
Card, blue and white paint, scissors, felt-tipped pen, adhesive, glitter.

Preparation
Make poster-sized copies of the poems the children created for Jack Frost, page 25.

What to do
Cover the wall with blue wallpaper or frieze paper. Ask the children to cut out triangle or icicle shapes from white card. The pieces need to resemble ice shards but the shapes needn't be too accurate as long as they are all straight and jagged, not curved.

Draw the outline of a huge Jack Frost on the backing paper and stick the shards of ice and frost all over the outline. Draw in some eyes and a mouth and any other features that will help to make the figure recognisable. Paint with splashes of blue and white. Put dabs of adhesive all over the figure and stick glitter to the adhesive.

Arrange the lines of the poem (from page 25) carefully around the picture. Pick out words the children know particularly well, for instance 'cold', 'frosty', 'shiver' and print them on jagged pieces of paper before sticking them around the picture.

Make paper card 'snowflakes' to hang in front of the frieze, put dabs of adhesive on them and let the children scatter glitter over the adhesive.

Give the board a title 'Jack Frost - on a cold and frosty morning'.

Discussion
Show the children the big picture you've made of Jack Frost, using their 'pieces of ice'. Encourage them to remember and talk about the Jack Frost drama. Who is Jack Frost? Where does he come from? What does he do? Is he real or pretend? How does he move about? What do you think he feels like if you touch him? What does it feel like to be him? Say: this is the poem the children wrote, can you find the words that say 'On a cold and frosty morning'. Who can remember all the poem? Who can join in if we read it together?

Round the mulberry bush

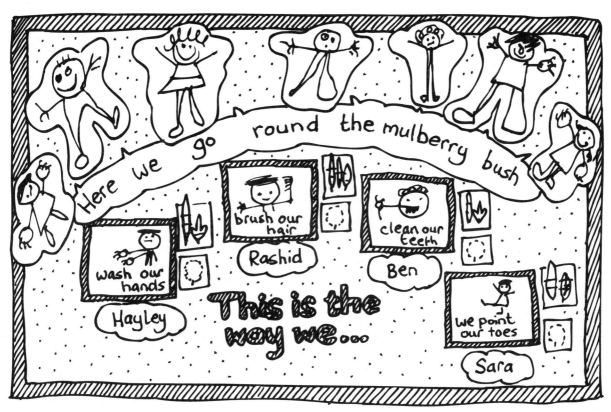

What you need
Frieze paper, card, paper, crayons.

Preparation
Cover the display space with wallpaper or frieze paper. Do the action rhyme together with lots of activities. Afterwards, ask each child to draw a large picture of an action or activity that they can do. Help them to write the words that describe the action underneath the picture.

Collect all the sewing cards from 'Sew a bush' page 29 and the weaving from 'Forest picture' page 32.

What to do
Fasten each child's activity picture to the wall, and try to put the same child's piece of sewing and piece of weaving close to it. Write each child's name on card, draw a thick felt-tipped pen bubble around the name and cut the bubble out, leaving the colour line intact.

Give the display a title 'This is the way we...'. Ask the children to draw and cut out a picture of themselves with their hands held out, as in the skipping circle. Fasten the pictures around the display. In a bubble, to denote singing, print the words: 'Here we go round the mulberry bush on a cold and frosty morning...'.

Discussion
Ask the children to locate their own pieces of work on the display. What letter begins their name? Does anybody else's name start with the same letter? Can they read their name? Invite them to tell you, and other people if possible, how they did their weaving. What did they collect? How did they do it? Do they remember the words – *up, down, front, back, through*? What did they do their sewing with? Can they remember how to do it? Can any of the children demonstrate the nursery rhyme to you/others/visitors, making up their own actions?

Frosty bushes

Group size
Small groups of three or four.

What you need
Half a packet of puffed rice cereal or cornflakes, 450g of chocolate, some desiccated coconut, icing sugar, little cake cases, large plate or cooking tin, two bowls, two spoons, hot water.

Preparation
Set the cake cases out on to the plate or cooking tin. Pour the hot water into one bowl and melt the chocolate over it, stirring all the time. It's better to do this part of the cooking without the children helping, because of the potential danger. Have the children wash and dry their hands.

What to do
Before the chocolate has time to set again, while it is still warm but not hot, let the children take turns to pour some of the cereal into it and stir it in carefully.

When the mixture is fairly stiff and you have added as much cereal as possible, help the children to spoon the mixture into the cake cases. Shape them into little bushes.

Next, help the children scatter desiccated coconut or icing sugar over the bushes to represent the frost. Leave the 'bushes' until the chocolate has set.

Discussion
Ask the children what they think will happen to the chocolate when it gets cold. Cereals aren't always used to make cakes, what do you usually eat cereal for? How do you prepare it to eat? How many cakes do you think you can make with one cupful of puffed rice?

Follow-up activities
▲ Show the children how to accurately weigh the chocolate and the cereal on small kitchen scales.
▲ Have a pretend 'Frosty Bush' shop and 'sell' the Frosty Bushes for a number of counters each. Let the children work out any 'change'.
▲ Have a tea-party with fruit juice and Frosty Bushes.
▲ After eating Frosty Bushes sing: 'This is the way we clean our teeth'! Use the opportunity to talk about other aspects of personal hygiene, such as washing hands.

▲ 38
Starting with rhyme
Action rhyme activities

Pat-a-Cake

Pat - a - cake, pat - a - cake, bak - er's man, Bake me a cake just as fast as you can.

Pat it and prick it and mark it with B, And put it in the ov - en for ba - by and me.

Pat-a-Cake is a clapping rhyme. The children clap their hands to the rhythm of the words, reciting it quite slowly.

When the children are good at clapping the rhythm introduce the idea of doing four quick little claps on the word 'fast'.

Some children may not know what the 'baker's man' is. Explain to them that baking is a special kind of cooking that we do in an oven. Baked foods are things like cakes, bread, biscuits, pastries and always use flour.

Before we used supermarkets every village had its own 'baker's shop' where the baker cooked bread and cakes, and often used huge ovens at Christmas to cook the villagers' Christmas turkeys and geese!

Many towns had several baker's shops and people either shopped for their bread daily or it was delivered to them by the 'baker's man'.

Lots of people bake at home and although they are not bakers in the 'shop' sense, they are still bakers because they are baking. Freshly baked food creates a delicious aroma that makes you feel quite hungry – perhaps the children have smelled the scent of newly-cooked bread wafting round the supermarket!

Since most children are interested in food, you can use the Pat-a-Cake rhyme and related activities as a stepping stone into a wider exploration of food – discussing meals they have during the day, when they eat them, their favourite foods, categories of foods, and so on.

If it is possible to visit a bakery shop, try to do so. In a supermarket the food is grouped in distinct sections, so the children will probably be familiar with the bakery counter but what do they think are the reasons for this kind of grouping? What is different about baked products compared with vegetables, meat, fish, dairy products or tinned foods?

The tasks in this section concentrate firmly on baking and clapping activities.

What can we buy?

Objective
English – to set up a bakery counter to provide a role-play activity.

Group size
Whole group.

What you need
Table-cloth, modelling dough, card, crayons, paper plates, boxes, play money, felt-tipped pen, magazine pictures of bakery items, bakery product packages.

Preparation
Set up the bakery counter on a corner table. Cover the table with a cloth. Use the modelling dough to make different shaped loaves, buns, biscuits and cakes (or use card). You could also cut pictures from magazines or use packages. Put all the items on to plates and into boxes, for displaying at the counter.

What to do
Ask the children the names of their favourite bakery items, provide any which they can't remember. Print each name which they suggest on a separate piece of card. With the children, think up a price for each item and write that on the card as well. Put each card beside the dough item/box or picture of what is being depicted.

Make several short lists, using only three or four items for each list, showing the items and their prices. Stand the lists up on the bakery counter or fasten them to the wall behind it.

Let the children 'shop' at the counter – matching the words from the lists with the words on the plates or by the boxes.

Discussion
Talk about some of the items you might find at the bakery counter such as: bun, roll, pie, custard tart, jam tart, small loaf, large loaf, sliced loaf, crusty bun, soft roll, biscuit, sandwich, cheese straw, tea cake, crumpet, waffle and pizza. Point out and focus on the sounds and letters that the children know or are learning.

For younger children
Limit the amount of items you have on the counter to just a few to begin with. Add more items, once they are familiar with the first few.

For older children
Encourage them to use the play money to pay for their items, and to work out the cost of what they're buying.

Follow-up activities
▲ Make 'jam tart' books. Cut the covers and pages in the shape of a jam tart and have the children colour a jam tart on the front. On the inside they can draw and write the word for one different item per page.

▲ Visit a local bakery counter with the children and buy one or two items.

▲ Write a 'list poem' together about things you can buy at the bakery.

▲ Play 'We went to the baker's and bought...' in a circle, with each child adding another item to the list.

Who for?

Objective
English – to develop letter and word recognition skills.

Group size
Four or five children.

What you need
A set of plastic letters, a class-made bakery counter with lots of different items, packages from bakery items, pictures of bakery items.

Preparation
Set up all the different bakery items on the counter or counters, so that they can be seen clearly. Make sure the children know the names of all the items such as: pie, loaf, jam tart, doughnut, bun, waffle, crumpet and muffin. Put the plastic letters into a bag.

What to do
Without looking into the bag the children take turns to pick a letter out and name it. Then they have to see what they can buy from the bakery counter using the letter to 'pay' for it, finding an item that begins with its sound.

Discussion
Encourage the children to identify all the things on the counter by name. What sound does each one begin with? What sound does it end with? What sounds can you hear in the middle?

For younger children
Leave difficult letters, such as 'x', out of the bag. Make sure the letters that are in the bag have an item on the counter to match with them.

For older children
If they pull out a letter like 'x' which obviously will not be the beginning of any of the words, ask them instead if they can see something that uses the sound of that letter for example 'box'.

Follow-up activities
▲ Play a game where one child chooses six letters at a time and places them on six different objects. The rest of the children have to decide whether the letters are on the right objects or not. If not, the child who knows better should move the letter to something that is right.
▲ Write cards with the first and second letter of each item. Hold up a card and give the children guesses at what the item is, for example. 'ja' for 'jam tart'. Progress to doing the same kind of thing with ending letters.

Match the cake

Objective
Mathematics – to learn the properties of simple shapes.

Group size
Four children.

What you need
Card, coloured felt-tipped pens, scissors.

Preparation
Introduce simple shapes – circle, triangle, square, rectangle. Cut the card into 24 pieces each about 6cm x 6cm. On the 24 cards, draw six each of the four shapes and cut them out. These represent the 'cakes'.

What to do
Keep one set of 'cake' shapes aside and put these pieces into a bag or an envelope. Spread all the other shapes on the table.

Invite each child to take a 'cake' from the bag without looking. They have to describe their shape verbally, saying how many sides/corners it has, and anything else they can observe about it. Now ask them to find all the other shapes to match theirs.

Discussion
Talk about what is the same and what is different about the shapes. Are the sides of the rectangle the same as the sides of the square? How many sides has the triangle? Are the corners the same? What's different about the circle?

For younger children
Use the 'cakes' for counting and for simple adding and subtracting. Share the 'cakes' amongst the children and count how many they can have each. Limit the number of cakes to five.

For older children
Write down the names of the shapes and refer to them constantly so that the children become familiar with how the shape names look as well as sound. Make little books with pictures of different shapes and their names for the children to refer to.

Follow-up activities
▲ Put all the shapes together into the bag so that they can't be seen and give the children turns to find a named shape without looking.
▲ Introduce the words: round, circular, triangular, rectangular.
▲ Make 'cakes' from different coloured card, or colour them differently, to introduce more properties.
▲ Make repeating patterns with the cakes (square, triangle, circle, rectangle, square, triangle...) and invite the children to continue them.

How much?

Objective
Mathematics – to develop concepts of bigger than and smaller than.

Group size
Up to six.

What you need
Mix for play dough (in proportions of two mugs plain flour/one mug of salt/dessertspoon of cooking oil, water), cool oven, powder paint.

Preparation
With the children, make up the play dough: mix together the dry ingredients and add water a little at a time to make the dough. Let the children form and pat the dough into lots of cakes of varying sizes. Ask them to each prick their initial on their cakes. Bake in a cool oven until they are hard and then paint them. The cakes can be covered with polyurethane varnish when the paint is dry.

What to do
Place all the completed 'cakes' together. Let the children work as a group to sort them in to size order – beginning with the smallest. They can then sort them in to order beginning with the biggest. They might also suggest other ways to sort them beginning with the fattest or the thinnest, the heaviest or the lightest.

Discussion
Compare the cakes. Which one is biggest of all? Which one is smallest of all? Which one is just a little bit bigger than the smallest? Pick up individual cakes. Which are smaller than this one? Which are bigger than this one? Which is fatter than this one?

For younger children
Help them to make sure they don't make all their cakes the same size. They can make 'one as small as the teeniest mouse', 'one as big as the fluffiest cat' and so on.

For older children
When they're making their cakes give them instructions to make: a small one, one a tiny bit bigger, one a bit bigger than that, a big one, and a huge one.

Follow-up activities
▲ Teach measuring words by using the children themselves, their feet, their clothing, toys as examples of relative size.

▲ Compare sizes – I saw a goldfish *this* big; I saw an ant *this* tiny and so on.

▲ When the children have finished the sorting activities, ask them to display their cakes in order and label them small/smaller/smallest, and so on.

▲ Do photocopiable page 91, 'How many' to practise simple counting and addition skills.

▶ **activities** ◀

Grow a name

Objective
Science – to mark the children's initials by growing cress.

Group size
Two or three children at a time.

What you need
Margarine tubs, mustard and cress seed, compost or cotton wool, pencil.

Preparation
Make sure the children all know how to make the shape of their initial and can do it without a problem. Let them practise with dry sand or lentils or another material that flows easily.

What to do
Tip some compost (or damp cotton wool will work) into each margarine tub and water it well. Share out the seeds amongst the children and help each child to trace (dibble) their initial using the pencil, into the compost. Carefully sow the seeds into the dibbled space.

Leave the pots on a windowsill and watch for the cress to grow. If the tubs look as if they are drying out, give them a spot of water.

Discussion
Talk about how things grow. Do you grow? Can you *feel* growing? How do you know you have grown? What do you need to make you grow? What do plants need?

For younger children
Help them to label their pots with their names, so that they don't get muddled up.

For older children
Observe and compare the growth between pots every day. Move the pots around occasionally, to see if more or less light makes a difference to the growth.

Follow-up activities
▲ Observe the cress each day to see if it's making progress. Keep a picture/word diary of the growth of the cress.
▲ Try growing other things – a carrot top will grow leaves if it's placed in a saucer of water. Try a parsnip, swede and leaf cuttings – succulents grow well from leaves.
▲ Make sandwiches with the cress.

▲
44
Starting with rhyme
Action rhyme activities

Name badges

Objective
Design and Technology – to make badges with the children's initials on.

Group size
Up to six children.

What you need
Small pieces of card, felt-tipped pens, sticky coloured paper, sticky tape, scissors.

Preparation
Remind the children of the rhyme. In the rhyme the baker marks the cake with B for Baby. Tell the children they are going to make their own cake badge with their initials on. Draw cake shapes on the cards. Ensure the children know what their initials are and how to write them.

What to do
Help the children to decorate their cakes with pieces of sticky coloured paper to represent icing, cherries and other decorations and then to mark the cakes with their initials using the felt-tipped pens. They can then cut the cake out.

Fold the sticky paper over to make it double-sided. The children can fix their badges to their clothes, their pencil cases, their books, or their bags.

At the end of the day, or session, collect all the initial badges and make sure they are kept in your care, so that the children don't venture outside wearing them. Tell the children you will be using them for a display (see page 53) later.

Discussion
Talk about the letters as you help them write. What does B stand for? What does T say in your name, Tom? How do you do a T? Where do you start? Let's start at the top and come down, making a stick, then go back to the top and put another stick across and so on.

For younger children
Young children might find it easier to cut a straight or circular shape around the cake than to try to follow the edges of the cake. Draw a felt-tipped pen line around the outside for them to follow with the scissors.

For older children
When the badges are all cut out, but before you stick the sticky tape to them, invite the children to sort out who the badges belong to by reading the letters.

Follow-up activities
▲ Make an alphabet frieze. Draw block letters of the alphabet, let the children colour them in. Cut them out and ask them to help you arrange them in alphabetical order and stick them with double-sided sticky tape.
▲ Stick envelopes to the frieze, one for each letter. Ask the children to cut out pictures or words that begin with that letter and put them in the right envelope.

Bringing the bread

Objective
History – to find out how bread used to be delivered.

Group size
Whole group.

What you need
Lots of space.

Preparation
Talk about how bread is made, and where we get it from. Most children will probably know the supermarket as the source of bread. Explain, that not very long ago, bread used to be bought at the baker's shop or delivered by the baker. The baker came in a van full of different kinds of bread and cakes, opened up the van at the back, piled bread and cakes into a huge bread basket and knocked on the door to see what the housewife wanted to buy.

What to do
Have the children in small groups, some to be housewives, some to be bakers. Let them improvise/pretend that the baker is coming with the bread in the basket to see what they want to buy.

After the improvisation, sit the children in a circle and you begin, '*The baker brings the bread. He knocks at the door...*' and the child next in the circle says '*...and I ask for one (whatever)*'. The next child says '*...and I ask for one (whatever it was), and two (something different)...*'. And so on, round the circle.

Discussion
Talk about what was different about the baker coming to the door, from buying bread today. Do you think the bread was the same? Was it wrapped in plastic film? Was it sliced? Was there so much variety? What reasons can you give for your ideas? If you could choose which would you have – delivery rounds or supermarkets? Why?

For younger children
Encourage them to play 'bakers' in the home corner. Show them the process of making the dough and cooking the bread, and then how to organise 'deliveries'.

For older children
Get them to sharpen up their improvisations until they can build them into little storylines or dramas which they can present to the rest of the group.

Follow-up activities
▲ Encourage the children to talk to their grandparents or great grandparents to find out ways in which daily life has changed.
▲ Write list poems of 'The baker brings the bread...' game.
▲ Take a trip to the local baker's or supermarket bakery for observation. Record the trip by making 'We went to the baker's' information books.

Starting with rhyme
Action rhyme activities

Where is it?

Objective
Geography – to record a plan of an imaginary place where the 'baker's shop' could be.

Group size
Four or five children.

What you need
Paper, pencils, crayons or felt-tipped pens, card, black felt-tipped pen.

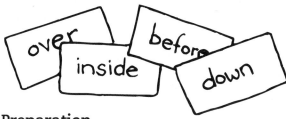

Preparation
Use a black felt-tipped pen to make a list of words on the card, include 'over' 'under', 'through', 'across', 'inside', 'outside', 'before', 'after', 'round', 'down', 'up'. Cut the words out to make flashcards and put them into a bag. The children will all need paper and pencils.

What to do
Tell the children that you are going to tell them a story and that they have to find out where the baker's shop is. Tell them to start by drawing a picture of a house in one corner of their paper.

Begin the story by saying, 'Dad wanted to buy some bread. He had to get to the baker's shop. He went...' pause and pull one of the words from the bag and show it to the children. Help them to read it and tell you what might come next. For example, if the word is 'down' they might say 'down the path'. They then draw the path.

Pull out another word, it might be 'through' and the children could suggest 'through the woods'. They can then draw the woods. The process continues until Dad has 'travelled' all the way from the house to the baker's shop.

When the pictures are finished and coloured in, ask the children to verbally trace Dad's journey. This will help to develop their geographical vocabulary.

Discussion
What would happen if you put all the words back in the bag and started again? Would you get the same journey?

For younger children
Restrict the words to six, so that the children don't run out of space on their paper.

For older children
Do the exercise again and find out how many different journeys they can draw. When they have had a couple of successful attempts, let them try writing the words rather than drawing the pictures.

Follow-up activities
▲ Draw a simple map of a journey which the children know, and encourage them to verbalise it, using the place words.

▲ Make another bag of words, this time with nouns - 'bridge', 'underpass', 'steps', 'river', 'street', 'crossing', and so on and play the same kind of game.

▲ Do photocopiable page 92 'Follow the paths' to practise pencil control.

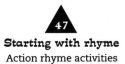

Fill up the counter

Objective
Art – to make some bakery items for the bakery counter activities.

Group size
Up to six children.

What you need
Paper, card, paints, felt-tipped pens, crayons, coloured sticky paper, scissors, pictures of bakery items and packages from a bakery.

Preparation
Have all the art materials organised in the centre of the table or space.

What to do
Tell the children that they are going to make some bakery items themselves. Show them the pictures you have collected and the bakery items and let them choose which item or items they want to make, and how they will make them.

Give them free choice for planning and making their items, helping and encouraging where necessary.

Discussion
Talk about what the children want to do. Let them describe what their item will look like. Ask them: how will you make it work? How will you show the cherry on the top? How do you know how big to make it? How

will you cut it out? How will you colour it? When the items are finished ask: is it how you wanted it? Can you think of a way to make it better? Can you make another one the same?

For younger children
Use sugar paper and card with younger children rather than painting paper which tends to tear easily. Make sure they know exactly what they want to do before they begin. Guide them in the right direction without actually telling them how to do it, so that they will have satisfaction from their efforts.

For older children
Encourage them to make specific sets of items, for instance, six cherry bakewells and ten jam doughnuts.

Follow-up activities
▲ Make play dough bakery items, using play dough (recipe on page 43).
▲ Help the children to write clear labels for their items.
▲ Make a montage of pictures cut from magazines and catalogues.
▲ Organise the children to do 'buying' and 'selling' of the bakery items.

What can you clap?

Objective
Music – to clap different rhythms and patterns.

Group size
Whole group.

What you need
Large space.

Preparation
Do the 'Pat-a-cake' rhyme lots of times so that the children have a good idea of clapping to the words and rhythm. Show them how they may clap using hand/hand, hand/knee, hands on partner's hands.

What to do
Practise Pat-a-cake several times with the children, once with ordinary clapping, once clapping the rhythm on knees, and once clapping hands with a partner.

Clap patterns for the children to follow, such as: slow, slow, fast, fast, slow or fast, fast, fast, slow, slow. Start with simple patterns to give the children confidence.

Clap the rhythms of different songs that the children already know, such as 'Here we go Round the Mulberry Bush', 'Ring-a-roses', 'Here-we-go-gathering-nuts in May', 'Hokey-cokey', and see if the children can guess which songs they are. Clap the songs with them using hand-clapping or hand/knee clapping or partner-clapping.

Discussion
How easy or hard is it to guess a tune from the rhythm? Can you clap a song for us to guess? Can you clap a new pattern for us all to follow?

For younger children
Give them plenty of time to try and follow the patterns that you clap. Keep the patterns simple and restrict them to hand clapping until they are confident with the pattern, because it's harder to make a clapping noise with hand/knee and partner-clapping.

For older children
Do the clapping patterns more quickly in succession. You clap a pattern, they respond, you clap another pattern, they respond, and so on. Try not to leave any gaps.

Follow-up activities
▲ Clap out the children's names which will help them to understand syllables.
▲ Play some music and try to clap the rhythm of it after listening for a short while.
▲ Play a game where clapping takes the place of some instruction. For example three fast claps mean stand up, two slow claps mean sit down, two fast claps, a beat and two more claps mean cross your legs!

▲ **49**
Starting with rhyme
Action rhyme activities

Making bread

Objective
PE – to use 'baking' as a starting point for exploring body shapes and movement.

Group size
Whole group.

What you need
Large space.

Preparation
Tell the children how bread is made. Explain that the baker has to mix the ingredients to make the dough and then kneads it thoroughly, stretching and pulling the dough with firm fingers and patting it with the heel of the hand to introduce air. The dough has to be left to rise and double its size, and the next step is to divide the dough into shape, and leave it to 'prove', when it doubles its size again.

What to do
Tell the children to imagine they are bakers and to get into the shape of a traditional baker. First, they are mixing the ingredients with a wooden spoon, next they must knead the dough, stretching it, pulling it, bashing it with the heel of their hands.

Now they can become the dough! Ask them to take their positions on the floor and feel themselves being pulled and stretched, pummelled and turned over and over. Pretend to break the dough and mould it into shapes, they could become crescent shapes, bun shapes, or long, thin roll shapes. They should lie as still as they can, then as slowly as possible puff themselves up as the dough rises. Ask them to start in a low, curled position, gradually stretching higher and wider, turning slowly on the spot.

Discussion
Get the children to demonstrate their actions. Who can show us how to be a baker? Who can show us how to pummel and pull the dough? Who can show us how to be dough? Who can show us how to be stretched and pulled as far as we can?

For younger children
Do follow-the-leader patterns of stretching and making shapes, asking the children to copy each other.

For older children
Ask them to develop their skills as bakers: getting the bread out of the oven, tapping the bottom to see if it is cooked properly, piling the bread up in the bread basket or on the shelves.

Follow-up activities
▲ Write and draw the baker's story.
▲ Make bread rolls with the children (see page 54, 'Baking bread').
▲ Ask the children to suggest as many cooking actions as they can: stirring, shaking, beating, patting into shape. Encourage the children to act them out, using their bodies to make different shapes.

Give a hand

Objective
RE – to focus on the 'hands clapping' to reinforce children's positive self-images.

Group size
Whole group.

What you need
Paper or card, felt-tipped pens, scissors.

Preparation
Practise the rhyme together, clapping hands as you go. Encourage the children to clap hands with each other as well as by themselves. Talk about all the good things they know about each other, remind them that no one is allowed to say anything negative, instead they must look for good points. Show them that hands are for friendship – we shake hands and hold hands, as well as clap, to show we are friends.

Discussion
Be ready to suggest positive comments that will boost each child's self image. Ask for anecdotes. Who has been extra helpful to someone this week? Who has shown friendship? Who has been kind to someone? Who has been generous in sharing?

For younger children
Talk about how we can all show caring and sharing with our friends, in our family and within the community. Lead them to see how caring and sharing becomes part of our nature and makes for a better society.

For older children
Help them to extend their positive images of themselves from five things, the fingers on one hand, to ten things, the fingers on both hands.

What to do
Show the children how to draw round one of their hands and help them to cut the hand shape out.

Ask each child to remember five positive words which other children have used to describe them. Let the children tell you the points and you can write one along each finger. Older children may be able to write the words themselves.

Make the hand shapes into a display.

Follow-up activities
▲ Make word labels for key words and use them on the hand picture with phrases that will help the children to think about how they are behaving. For example: have I been helpful today? Have I cared for someone today?
▲ Encourage the children to tell each other examples of caring and sharing they have experienced.
▲ Make flap books with the concept words and different names so that they are interchangeable.

Baker's shop

What you need
Backing paper, scissors, sticky tape, paper plates, doilies, word labels from page 40 'What can we buy?'.

Preparation
Cover the display space with some decorative or coloured paper to give it a solid backing.

The bakery items which the children have drawn, coloured and cut out will look more consistent if you mount them all on coloured sugar paper. Cut around them, leaving a margin of about 1 cm all the way around. Use just one colour for these frames.

What to do
Save one sample of each item, to go with the label. Stick the others on paper doilies and then on paper plates. Place the paper plates carefully on the space. Fasten the labels and sample in a list down the left hand side of the display.

Write questions, draw bubbles around them and cut them out. Stick these around the display. Questions you might write are: Can you see jam tarts? How many doughnuts can you see? Which is the biggest cake? Which is the smallest loaf? Try and find some biscuits. How many can you see? Where are the ginger snaps? Can you find the words that match?

Add further questions appropriate to the pieces of artwork you have. To finish the display off, place a small table at the front with real bakery items on, labelled and priced.

Discussion
Help the children to 'read' the questions and look for the answers. Where is your own piece of work? Can you match the pictures with the words and pictures on the list? Can you read any of the words? What does this sentence say? If you had one plate with one each of the cakes on it what would be on the plate altogether?

We care and share

What you need
Badges from 'Name badges' page 45, plans from 'Where is it?' page 47, hands from 'Give a hand' page 51. Card, felt, paper, staples or sticky tape, wall or frieze paper, coloured wool.

Preparation
Assemble all the pieces of work you have. Cover your display space with wallpaper or frieze paper. Print and cut out the words of the rhyme in large print, in two pieces. Leave big box spaces for the letter 'B' and for 'Baby'.

What to do
Fix the first two lines of the rhyme at the top of the display space, and the last two lines at the bottom.

Write the letters of the alphabet in capitals and put them with the initial badges to one side of the rhyme. Write a label saying: 'Find the letter that begins your name' and stick it somewhere by the alphabet letters.

Make a label which says: 'We care and share' and stick it in the centre of the right-hand space. Stick the hands so they look as if they are exploding out of it. If possible, back and frame the hands on sugar paper before you stick them in the space.

Connect each child's initial badge to their hand with lengths of coloured wool.

Discussion
Go through the letters of the alphabet. Join the badges and hands together with the help of the children, reinforcing the initial letters of their names as you go along. The spaces in the two boxes are so that children can take turns, once or twice a day, to choose somebody they would like to 'mark their cake for'. They choose the correct letter for their friend's name and help you to write the letter and the name on small pieces of card. Fix these into the spaces with screwed up sticky tape so that they are easy to remove for the next turn.

Baking bread

Group size
Three or four children at a time.

What you need
Three teaspoons dried yeast and one teaspoon castor sugar (or 28g fresh yeast), 1.5kg plain flour, 1½ pints warm water, five level teaspoons salt, 240g of self raising flour, 40g lard, small bowl, large warm bowl, floured surface, baking sheets, tea-towel, warm place.

Preparation
These ingredients will make enough dough for lots of children to make a bread roll each. If possible allow all the children in the group to watch you mixing the dough, but then divide the children into small groups of three or four to do the kneading and dividing. Make sure all the children have clean hands. Grease the baking sheets.

What to do
If using dried yeast, reconstitute it in the small bowl with a quarter of a pint of the warm water and the sugar, until it is frothy. If using fresh yeast, cream it with a little of the warm water.

Add the yeast mixture and the remainder of the water to the flour and mix, by hand, until the dough leaves the bowl cleanly.

Knead thoroughly, and let the children knead, on the floured surface.

Divide the dough and let the children shape it into small rolls or bun-shapes. Place them on the greased baking sheets.

Cover the rolls with the cloth and leave them in a warm place for 45–50 minutes to let them rise.

Bake in a hot oven, 225°C, gas mark 7-8, for 10–15 minutes.

Discussion
Why is it important to have the right weight of ingredients? What happens to the rolls when they are left in the warm place? Count the rolls. Are there enough for everyone to have one?

Follow-up activities
▲ Using the same recipe you can make loaves of bread. Divide the dough into two and place it in warm greased bread tins, pressing well into the corners, to make two large loaves. Cover them with a cloth and leave them to rise. Large loaves will take 45–50 minutes to cook.
▲ Make four small loaves by dividing the dough into four and fashioning it into round shapes. Put them onto the greased baking sheet and cover them, to rise. Small loaves will take about 35–40 minutes to cook.
▲ Use the bread to make sandwiches with the children.

chapter four
▶ introduction ◀

The Wheels on the Bus

1. The wheels on the bus go round and round, Round and round, round and round. The

wheels on the bus go round and round, All day long._____

The wheels on the bus go round and round
(Make circling or rolling movements with hands to rhythm)
Round and round, round and round,
(Circling or rolling movements with hands again)
The wheels on the bus go round and round
(Circling or rolling movements with hands again)
All day long.
The wipers on the bus go swish, swish, swish
(Make windscreen wiper movements with hands to rhythm)
The horn on the bus goes beep, beep, beep
(Make pressing horn movement with hands to rhythm)
The driver on the bus goes 'Move down the bus!' *(officiously)*
(Make ticking-off signals with finger to rhythm)
The mums on the bus go chatter, chatter, chatter
(Make busy, fast, chatter movements of head to rhythm)
The dads on the bus go doze, doze, doze *(sing slowly)*
(Make slow, nodding movements of head, eyes closed, to rhythm)
The children on the bus go rah, rah, rah *(noisy and fast)*
(Jump up and wave arms about as if playing wildly)

This is such a jolly rhyme, you can extend it by adding new lines and actions about almost anything! Make some lines up to fit  in with a topic you are working on, for example, if you were doing a topic about animals you could sing 'The lambs on the bus go baa, baa, baa' and so on. A topic about school could include the line 'The teachers on the bus say 'sit down nicely' for example.

The rhyme fits in very well with all subject areas and provides plenty of opportunities for all kinds of tasks and activities, including teaching some early road safety.

I'm on the bus

Objective
English – to help the children express themselves confidently and to aid memory.

Group size
Any size.

What you need
No special equipment, a comfortable place.

Preparation
It would be useful (though not essential) to take the group on a bus journey beforehand.

What to do
Sit the children in a circle and talk together about travelling on a bus. Let any children who travel on buses regularly tell the others about their experiences. Encourage them all to imagine they are on a bus. What can they see inside/outside the bus?

Ask them to choose a place where they could go on an imaginary bus trip. Ideally, make it somewhere the children all know so that they have a good idea of the journey the bus might take and what they might pass on the way. If you have all been on a bus trip together use that shared experience for the basis of the game.

Ask one child to begin, 'I'm going on the bus to town (or wherever). I can see...'. The next child repeats 'I'm going on a bus to town. I can see... and...' expanding the list and then continuing around the circle. Each child repeats the list and adds something extra. Try to ask the children to concentrate, first on things inside the bus, then on things outside the bus. Keep the game going for as long as the children can manage to remember the list.

Discussion
Talk about what's different about making journeys by foot, by car, by bus. Some children may never have been on a bus at all, whereas, to many, it's a regular adventure. There's quite a social difference between sitting in a car with your family and being with other people on a bus !

For younger children
Be ready to give clues to any child who has a problem, remembering the list. Encourage the other children to help in a friendly way. Maybe they can find, or point out, objects in your room that will help.

For older children
Make it more of a challenge by asking them to 'guess your secret'. You can choose a place to go (for example the town or the park), but don't tell the children and make sure what you can 'see' begins with the same letter or sound. Let the children offer ideas of things they can see. If their suggestions begin with the sound you are working on (for example 't' for town) then you 'let them go on the trip' but if their suggestions begin with something different then say 'sorry, they stay home'. One by one they will begin to discover your 'secret'.

Follow-up activities
▲ Make up a Big Book story together in the shape of a bus.
▲ Make a drama map of the journey your bus might go on, using sheets of paper on the floor.
▲ Make a collection of toys with wheels.
▲ Use circular lids for the children to draw round to make sets of wheels.
▲ Try photocopiable page 93 'Who's on the bus?' to develop vocabulary and aid memory.

Look out!

Objective
English – to make a safety awareness book.

Group size
Up to eight children.

What you need
Card, felt-tipped pens, crayons, pencils, white paper, stapler or sticky tape.

Preparation
Make sure that you stress that children under eight should not cross a road without an adult. Explain that when they are older they will use the Green Cross Code but now they must practise it with an adult.

Explain to the children that although the Green Cross Code helps you keep safe it does not provide a 'magic carpet'. Even at Pelican and Zebra crossings they must follow the rules. Check that the children understand the word 'kerb'. Ensure that the children understand that 'look around' means look for moving traffic – traffic may come from all directions and doesn't always make a noise. Explain that they must walk in a straight line across the road.

What to do
Explain that you are going to make a book to tell other people the Green Cross Code. Each book has six pages, with one rule per page. Ask the children to draw pictures, showing themselves following the rules. Print the words for each rule for the children to copy or provide dotted guide lines for them to complete on their pages. Help them to read the words back to you.

Put a front and back cover on each book and staple or stick them together.

Ask the children to draw traffic lights on the front, showing red for STOP and ask them to write their names on.

Discussion
Ask the children what kind of things move along the road. How can you tell if something is coming towards you or going away from you? Why should you cross the road calmly, not run? Why should you always walk across the road in a straight line? What places do you know that make it safer to cross?

For younger children
Make sure you don't alarm them with the dangers of road crossing. Stress the need to take care at all times, even with an adult.

For older children
Discuss with them why they shouldn't walk in the road, or play in the street. Make sure they have a basic 'street' vocabulary – pavement, road, kerb, traffic, pelican crossing and so on.

Follow-up activities
▲ Make maps and routes of the local area filling in safe and dangerous places to cross.
▲ Make 'sets' of things that move fast on the road.

How many wheels?

Objective
Mathematics – to develop concepts of counting and tallying.

Group size
Three or four.

What you need
Card, felt-tipped pen, scissors, adhesive.

Preparation
Cut out car, bicycle, bus, and lorry shapes from the card. The shapes can be very simple but make sure you provide a mixture of vehicles, some with two wheels, some four, some six or more. Cut out lots of sets of wheels in different sizes. For each child use an A4 sheet of paper, rule a line down the centre and write: 'How many wheels?' at the top of one column and 'How many vehicles?' at the top of the other.

What to do
Give each child an assortment of 'vehicles', the prepared sheet of paper and a pencil. They can choose to colour the vehicles before or after the counting activity. Place the wheels in sets according to size in the centre of the table.

Let the children each choose a vehicle on which they can fix wheels. How many wheels will each vehicle need? Which size

wheels? The children must take their wheels carefully, counting to make sure they have the right number. When they have the correct number they can stick the wheels to their vehicle. Show them that a bicycle will have two wheels and a car will have four, two each side of the card.

Help the children to glue their wheels on to their vehicles. Ask them to write the number of wheels for that vehicle in the first column and write '1' in the second column for the number of vehicles. They should draw a picture in this column to show whether it is a bike, car or a truck.

Discussion
Introduce the word 'vehicles' to the children. Do you know any other vehicles? What are they? Do all vehicles have wheels? Which vehicle has the most wheels? Which has the least? How many vehicles have you got at home? How many wheels do they have?

For younger children
Keep to low numbers. Help them to add up the number of vehicles they have at the end. First add up the number of vehicles column. Then add up the actual vehicles to which they have stuck wheels. Do they match?

For older children
Can they count their wheels out in pairs or twos? Help them to add up both columns and their vehicles; do the numbers match? How many wheels do they think they have used altogether? Do the numbers tally with the wheels on the vehicles?

Follow-up activities
▲ Learn some number rhymes such as, 'One potato, two potato'.
▲ Make a hopscotch game with big sheets of card with numbers on them. Show the children how to play.
▲ Try the photocopiable page 94, 'Wheels' to develop observation skills.

Circles everywhere

Objective
Mathematics – to look for round shapes inside and outside.

Group size
Whole group.

What you need
Your normal group environment with its equipment and resources.

Preparation
Talk about the 'wheels on the bus' being round. Explain that we call the round shape a 'circle'. Try some circle games, such as 'Ring a Ring o' Roses', 'Here we go Round the Mulberry Bush' (see page 23) and 'I Sent a Letter to my Love'.

What to do
Sit the children in a circle on the floor. One-by-one invite them to leave the group to find something in the room that is a circle. They can bring small objects to the group, or point to things that aren't moveable. Run your finger round the edge of all the circles to show them how the circle seems to go round without a beginning and without an end.

Go round the sitting circle again and ask each child to think of something they know that has a circle (mug, cup, saucer, plate, tin of food and so on).

Discussion
Why do the children think wheels need to be round? Have you seen wheels another shape? Would wheels work if they were another shape? Why not?

For younger children
Help the children to notice the circles they are playing with. For instance, when they are playing in the sandpit or in the water tray help them to notice the circles on yoghurt pots, buckets or jugs.

For older children
Instead of bringing their objects to the sitting circle, invite older children to draw their ideas and show them, explaining to the group what their objects are and where they can see the circles.

Follow-up activities
▲ Draw a large chalk circle outside and ask the children to tiptoe, hop or skip around its edges. Do the same with a figure 8.
▲ Make a circle caterpillar. Each child needs a paper plate, or something to draw round and cut out. Cut out lots of circles and overlap them in a long wiggly line on the wall, make a face at one end and put two feet on each circle.
▲ Cut circles in potatoes and do potato and cotton reel prints.

Slow down!

Objective
Science – to experiment with wheels and objects without wheels.

Group size
Four or five children.

What you need
Wheeled toys, balls, cylinders, small blocks, large blocks, a sheet of plywood/hardboard/heavy card, two large sheets of paper, felt-tipped pens.

Preparation
Divide one sheet of writing card into three columns, labelled 'Whose turn', 'What with' and 'What happened'. Collect all the toys together. Arrange the large blocks with the hardboard leaning against it to make an incline. Place the second large sheet of paper on the floor in front of it.

What to do
Let the children each choose a toy or block. They can take turns to let their chosen object slide or roll down the incline. Tell them not to push the toy just to let go of it. Mark on the paper with a felt-tipped pen the spot on the ground where the object reaches.

Fill in the columns on the first sheet, with the children helping. They should be thinking about 'fast', 'slow', 'direction' and 'how far'.

When they have each had one turn let them choose another object. They should try to predict whether this one will go faster or slower than their first attempt and whether it will go further or not so far.

Continue the investigation until you have tried all the objects.

Discussion
Ask the children to predict what will happen with the same objects if they push them instead of just letting go. What will happen if you make the incline steeper or not so steep? What will happen to the objects if you try to make them go up the board instead of down? Investigate to see how close their predictions are.

For younger children
Just try objects that have wheels to start with, then try the same investigations with objects that don't have wheels, such as cylinders or balls. Try again with objects that are not round at all, such as cubed blocks.

For older children
Ask older children to keep their own record sheets, using the first column to predict what will happen, the second column to show what actually happened and the third to compare the two.

Follow-up activities
▲ Try using the same objects with the board flat on the floor. Do the children have to use more force to make the objects move?
▲ Do balancing investigations by lying the hardboard across some of the blocks and inviting the children to balance the two ends with the toys.
▲ Organise a game where the children roll the objects down the board to see whose goes furthest. Ask the children not to use any 'push' to keep the test 'fair'.

Who's on the bus?

Objective
Design and Technology – to make finger puppets of the people on the bus.

Group size
Four or five children.

What you need
Card, scissors, sticky tape, crayons, oddments of textured paper or fabric, adhesive.

Preparation
Sing through the rhyme together. Let the children decide whether they would like to make a driver or a passenger finger puppet. Cut the card into pieces about 8cm x 4cm, and into strips 2cm x 5cm.

What to do
Help the children to each draw and cut out a rough shape – 6 or 7cm tall by 3cm wide.

The children can then draw and colour their choice of person on one side of the card, they can add pieces of textured paper or fabric and wool for hair and so on.

When the person puppet is finished, make a small ring from one of the strips to roughly fit the child's finger. Attach the ring with sticky tape to the back of the puppet. The children can then wear their puppets facing into the palm of the hand so that they can be wiggled.

Discussion
Ask the children to work in pairs to have a conversation with their puppets 'talking' to each other. Where are you going on the bus? What are you going to do when you get there? What's your name? Tell me about yourself.

For younger children
The puppets can get quite fiddly if the children attempt to be too accurate. They can be quite simple but still provide valuable imaginative play. Help with the difficult parts such as sticking on hair.

For older children
Instead of drawing and colouring their puppets, they might like to cut and glue the whole thing. Provide coloured sticky paper from which to cut eyes, mouths, clothes and even buttons.

Follow-up activities
▲ Make whole 'families' of finger puppets.
▲ Encourage the children to tell 'stories' of their 'journeys' using the finger puppets.
▲ Make animal finger puppets in the same way and do a story about a ride on a bus to a farm or zoo.
▲ Get the children to make up names and histories for their finger puppets. Make little books about them. Fix the finger puppet into a pocket stuck on to the front.

▲ 61
Starting with rhyme
Action rhyme activities

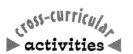

No wheels

Objective
History – to think about how life might have been before wheels were invented.

Group size
Whole group.

What you need
Lots of space.

Preparation
Tell the children they are all going to act out a story of long, long ago, before there were any wheels in the world. Explain that you will tell them the story, and they can do the actions as you go along.

What to do
Tell the children to each find a space to sit in and to close their eyes while you tell them a story.

Begin... *Long, long ago, when the world was very young, no one had discovered wheels. There was no transport. No buses, or cars, or bikes. There were no wheels in the whole world.*

The children can pretend to sleep in their caves. When the sun rises it peeps into the cave and wakes them up. On waking, they don't have to get dressed because they wear the same things all the time. But they need to wash, and have a drink. So they have to trudge off to the nearest river. All the babies and little children have to be carried. Some of the cave people go back to the cave with the children, to light the fire. On the way, they collect rocks to build up the door to their cave, or for furniture. It all has to be carried. The others go off, hunting for food. When they find a wild animal for food they have to carry and drag it back to the cave where it's cooked and eaten.

Simplify/extend the story to suit your group. Avoid suggesting that people used to pick and eat vegetation, for safety reasons.

Discussion
Encourage the children to tell you what they think are the differences between life long ago, and now. Once the wheel was invented what difference do you think it made? What things could they do?

For younger children
Before younger children learn about the distant past, they will need to have plenty of time to learn about the circular cycle of the day beginning with the sun rising and then setting, through to night time and then the sun rising again.

For older children
Encourage them to work out as many changes as they possibly can between this time long ago and today. Start with life today and work out what the children would miss about it.

Follow-up activities
▲ Ask the children to move something heavy, such as sand, without using wheels.
▲ Make wheel tracks: place sheets of paper on the ground outside, and position a large piece of paint-filled sponge nearby. Ask the children to wheel or ride their wheeled vehicles through the paint and across the paper to make tracks.
▲ Make an obstacle course outside for the children to ride through.

Starting with rhyme
Action rhyme activities

Where shall we go?

Objective
Geography – to plan an imaginary bus route.

Group size
Four or five children.

What you need
A large sheet of paper, felt-tipped pens.

Preparation
Ask the children to think where they would like to go on a pretend trip on a bus. They may suggest somewhere 'real'; encourage them to make up a fantasy name for it so that they don't get confused when they're planning their route or ask them to create their 'own' place. The drawing only needs to be simple, it can be as easy as drawing shaped blocks or spaces.

What to do

Draw your destination on the top or bottom right-hand corner of the sheet of paper and label it.

Tell the children you are going to start the imaginary journey from 'home' in the diagonally opposite corner. Draw 'home' and label it. Explain that you now have to fill in all the rest of the paper, to make your map. What kind of things would they like on the map? Where should these things go? Help the children to decide and give cues: 'Do we need a school?', 'Do we need some shops?' 'Shall we have a train station?' 'Shall we have a river?' for example. Add some new things on the map that may not be in their own environment, to widen their horizons. Include some road signs.

When all the places on the map are drawn, concentrate on the bus route. Make the bus route in a different colour and make it as twisty as possible to incorporate all the different places on the map.

Discussion
Help the children to use as many place and direction words as possible: *over*, *through*, *left*, *behind* and so on. Encourage them to repeat the words and ask 'where did you say?' frequently so that they use them in a functional way. Do you remember any road signs that you may have seen?

For younger children
Keep the plan quite simple. Label everything as you go along with clues that will help them. For instance, although you may draw a bubble shape for a wood, write the word 'wood' in it and draw a tree. Help them to trace the journey with their fingers, verbalising the route as they go along.

For older children
Allow them to do most of the planning and problem-solving, just give them cues if they get stuck. Encourage them to think about why certain things might be near others, for instance, why a school might be near a housing estate.

Follow-up activities
▲ Divide the route into small square sections, number them. Let the children take turns to throw dice and move a number of sections, until they get to the destination.
▲ Write the story of the journey and what happens when the children arrive.
▲ Show the children simple maps and trace routes on them.

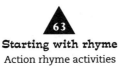

▲ 63
Starting with rhyme
Action rhyme activities

Busy street

Objective
Art – to make a busy street montage.

Group size
Whole group.

What you need
Lots of coloured magazines, scissors, adhesive, wheel stencils, one colour of paint, paint brushes, large sheet of card

Preparation
Draw a margin around the edge of the card, about 10 or 12cm wide. Cut out the wheel stencils from card. Draw the wheels, with lots of spokes to make an interesting stencil shape and cut them out. Tell the children you are going to make a montage of a busy street or even a busy town. The street will be in the centre, and the wheel stencils will be all round the edges.

What to do
Help the children to look through the magazines, looking for pictures of things that would be found in the street, such as cars, bikes, trees, people, street signs and so on. Help them cut out their pictures.

Let the children decide where to put their individual cut-out pictures and then stick them in place on the large sheet of card, inside the frame. They can then go and look for another suitable picture.

Don't worry about trying to make a 'picture'. The idea of the montage is to fill up all the space in a colourful, busy way. Some of the pictures may even have to overlap. Fill in any spaces with paint.

Help the children to place the wheel stencils in the margins and paint in the spaces to match the montage background.

Discussion
Find a good selection of items. Ask them to find specific things when the montage is complete. Can you find a motor-cycle? Can you find a policeman? Can you find a bike? What else might we see in the street? When the montage is finished, ask the children to locate their own cut-outs.

For younger children
Let them cut one thing out and stick it, at a time. Give plenty of help with the cutting out and spacing of cut-outs on the card. Talk them through the whole activity, ask is that one too close to the next one? Is the space too big? Is the space too small? Can we cut a nice clear edge round this car?

For older children
Give them clear instructions to remember. 'Look for a car, a bus, two people and a signpost'. When they bring their cut-outs to you, ask them which they have managed to collect and which they couldn't find, to check what they have remembered.

Follow-up activities
▲ Ask the children to make small montages of their own, choosing their own subjects.
▲ Cut out different stencil shapes to decorate other artwork, or books. Use montage to make book covers.
▲ Talk about 'what could cause an accident' and locate danger spots in the environment.

Listen for the bus

Objective
Music – to make music for 'The wheels on the bus'.

Group size
Whole group.

What you need
Percussion instruments, or home-made instruments.

Preparation
Make sure the children can all sing and clap 'The wheels on the bus' rhyme.

What to do
Give each child a musical instrument. Provide simple instruments:
▲ cut lengths of dowelling to tap together;
▲ tap wooden spoons/empty yoghurt pots/ blocks together;
▲ hit card boxes or tins with a stick or wooden spoon;
▲ fix sandpaper to two blocks and rub them briskly together;
▲ string up several plant pots and tap them with a spoon or stick;
▲ tie spoons to a long length of string, to shake and jangle;
▲ put dried peas/rice/gravel into empty washing-up bottles or different shaped and sized containers to shake (ensure that you stick the lids on securely);
▲ hand different lengths of thin wood from the back of a chair to tap with a stick;
▲ secure rubber bands round a brick or box to twang.
   The children can sing the rhyme through using their musical instruments in time with the rhythm.

Discussion
How can the children all keep together? How can you make sure you begin together, keep in time, and end together? Which instruments give similar sounds? Which instrument do you like using best?

For younger children
Rehearse plenty of times to establish starting and stopping on cue before the final version. Give clear signals, and keep everybody watching you as you conduct.

For older children
Divide the children into different groups to take turns to sing and play. Give them clear instructions and help them to remember when it is their turn.

Follow-up activities
▲ Swap the instruments around so that everybody gets the chance to have a go with each one.
▲ Make a cassette recording of traffic driving past, speeding up, slowing down, braking, and ask the children to listen and decide what's happening from the sounds.
▲ Record the children singing and playing and play the tape back to them.

Bus drivers

Objective
PE – to explore contrasts of speed, shape, direction and level.

Group size
Whole group.

What you need
Large space.

Preparation
Make sure the children know how to stop on command, and how to move around the space without bumping into each other.

What to do

Begin with the children all pretending to be the driver of the bus, turning the steering wheel. Can they go straight ahead and left and right, moving at a normal walking pace? Now let them try to be the wheels of the bus, rolling on the floor. Can they roll straight ahead, left, right and backwards?

The children need to stand up again, to be the driver working out a pathway. Lead the children in a follow-my-leader line, using slow, controlled travelling actions to establish a pathway. The pathway might be in a long straight line, with a sudden sharp turn to face a new direction, or a short, zigzagging pathway, a curved or twisting line, weaving in and out, a circle, or a spiral pathway. Choose each pathway carefully.

When the children understand the pathways, ask them to march, hop, run, skip, slither, creep, jump and tiptoe in the different pathways. End with them choosing a pathway and level of their own, keep the speed slow so that they don't bump into each other.

Discussion
Invite the children to demonstrate that they understand different words. Who can show us a tiptoe? Who can show us a crawl, a slither, a scurry, a trot, a creep, a march? Who can show us some circle movements – twirl, whirl, spin, roll, twist, curl? Who can show pathway words – zigzag, straight, left, right, curve, twist, spiral?

For younger children
Stick to just a few words at a time, and repeat the same patterns over and over again. Choose different children to be the leader and give positive encouragement.

For older children
Aim for high quality movement and comment positively on really expressive shapes or clear movements so that the others will observe and mimic.

Follow-up activities
▲ Use percussion instruments to stimulate the movements, for instance, gentle shaking of a tambourine, or short, sharp tapping.
▲ Play tightrope walking using chalk to draw long pathways on the ground. Suggest to the children they are balancing on a tightrope and get them to tiptoe the lines.
▲ Make spirals out of card: cut a circle, begin from the centre drawing round and round until you reach the edge. Cut along the line and shake the spiral out.

Signs for safety

Objective
RE – to identify street signs in order to look after oneself and others in a safe way.

Group size
Five or six.

What you need
An outside observation point.

Preparation
Talk to the children about accidents, how they happen, and how they can be avoided.

What to do
Organise the children to go to the school/nursery gates with you and together look for:
▲ school gates, to stop the children running out into the road;
▲ signs outside the school, to slow the traffic down;
▲ road markings, to stop traffic parking where children might be crossing;
▲ traffic passing the school, it should be driving slowly;
▲ any provision for crossing, pelican crossing or lollipop person.

Back inside, talk about what you have seen while you were outside.

Discussion
Talk to the children about how they come to and go home from your group. Who collects you? Is there a lollipop person? How do you know when it is safe to cross the road? Make sure they know and understand the Green Cross Code.

For younger children
Impress on the children that 'looking around' to see if anything is coming, is not enough. They should be looking out for traffic coming and listening for traffic coming with their parent/helper.

For older children
How many other signs do they know? Ask them to look out for and remind each other of signs. Can they draw and describe them to the rest of the group?

Follow-up activities
▲ Make a large Green Cross Code poster, drill the children in learning it.
▲ Make a frieze to show the children coming to your group and crossing safely.
▲ Draw pictures and label them of people who help the children cross roads safely.

Our street

What you need
Backing paper, montage from 'Busy street' page 64, card, felt-tipped pen, scissors, staples, sticky tape.

Preparation
Back the wall with frieze or wallpaper. Stick the montage on some card or sugar paper, leaving a frame all the way round it and mount it in the middle of the wall space.

What to do
Give the montage a heading 'Busy street'. Make some labels, saying: This is a busy street. Can you cross it safely? Look for cars, moving traffic, lorries, buses, bicycles, the kerb, pedestrian crossing, lollipop person, pelican crossing. Make a poster, saying: What to do, Find a safe place to stop, Stand on the pavement near the kerb, STOP at the kerb, Look all around and listen, Let the traffic pass, Look around again, Walk straight across the road, Look and listen for traffic as you cross.

Illustrate the labels with small drawings to make them more eye-catching and arrange these around the montage. If you have room, place a table or box to the front of the display where you can show the children's own Road Safety books from 'Look out!', page 57.

Discussion
Read out the words and labels as often as you can. Ask the children to read the labels with you, pointing to each word in turn. Even if they are not yet able to read they will eventually pick up the messages and will begin to remember them in the right order. Ask them to look for specific words on the display. Can you see 'stop'? Can you find 'safe'? Show me the traffic/crossing.

Round and round

What you need
Card, paper, paints, vehicles from 'How many wheels?', page 58, ideas from 'Circles everywhere', page 59 and finger puppets from 'Who's on the bus?' page 61.

Preparation
Draw and cut out a huge bus shape from card. Ask the children to do a self-portrait and cut it out. Collect all the items to be displayed together.

What to do
Stick the bus into the middle of the space available. Stick the children's self-portraits on to the bus, as passengers and drivers.

Make a large label: 'The wheels on the bus go round and round all day long' and stick it to the bottom half of the bus, or below the bus.

Make another label saying 'Circles – wheels are round, they are circles' and stick it to the left of the bus. Make labels to show the things that the children found in the classroom which were circles, and stick them down this side.

Stick labels saying 'How many wheels?' and 'How many vehicles can you count?' to the right of the bus. In between the two labels stick all the vehicles. Position the finger puppets around the top of the display. (If you put them near the bottom they may not last very long as little hands will want to remove them and play with them!)

Discussion
Reinforce the concept words – circle, wheel, round, vehicle. Talk the children through the labels, pointing to each word. Can you see what Tom found? Can you see what Rashed found? Who can find me the word 'circle'? Who can see the word 'wheel'? Who can see the word 'bus'? Can anyone see the word 'vehicle'? Who can explain what a vehicle is? You can count the wheels, the people on the bus and the finger puppets.

Wheels to eat

Group size
Four or five children.

What you need
100g butter, 50g castor sugar, 150g plain flour, basin, rolling pin, pastry cutter, wooden spoon, palette knife, blunt knife, baking sheet, wire rack.

Preparation
Assemble all the equipment and ingredients. Flour the baking sheet. Turn the oven on to 170°C, gas mark 3. Make sure the children have clean hands.

What to do
Cream the butter thoroughly with the wooden spoon. Add the sugar and beat together until light and fluffy. Add half the flour and mix well. Add the remaining flour and mix to a dough. Knead the dough lightly to make it smooth. Roll it out thinly, about 0.25 cm thick. Cut into rounds. Mark spokes on the 'wheels' with a blunt knife.

Use the palette knife to transfer the biscuits to the baking sheet. Bake for about twenty minutes. Leave to cool on the rack.

Discussion
Talk about what happens to the butter when it's creamed. What happens when you add the sugar to it? What happens when you add the flour? Let the children all have a turn at stirring during the different stages so that they can feel the difference in the texture and pliability.

Follow-up activities
▲ Ask the children to help with all the clearing up and washing up.
▲ Use this recipe to make other biscuits by adding some dried fruit, or decorate them with icing or sweets. You can also prick names or initials into them instead of wheel spokes.
▲ Use the biscuits for counting and subtracting activities: 'There were ten on the tray how many are left if one is eaten?'.

▶ **introduction** ◀

I Hear Thunder

I hear thun - der, I hear thun - der, Hark don't you? Hark don't you?

Pit - ter pat - ter rain drops, Pit - ter pat - ter rain drops. I'm wet through, So are you.

I hear thunder, I hear thunder,
(Children stamp feet in rhythm)
Hark, don't you? Hark, don't you?
(Children put hands behind ears in listening pose)
Pitter patter raindrops, pitter patter raindrops,
(Children make pitter-patter movements with their hands in the air before them)
I'm wet through, So are you!
(Children hug themselves to signify wet and cold).

I Hear Thunder is a singing and action rhyme, sung to the tune of Frère Jacques. The children can join in with accompanying actions to reinforce the words.

The song has lots of potential for learning about the weather, as well as for work on different sounds. It provides a good opportunity for small children to try and remember what types of weather are associated with various times of the year which can lead towards an understanding of the changing seasons.

Many children are frightened of thunderstorms and this rhyme can provide good opportunities for trying to allay those fears. Explain to the children what it is that makes the banging and causes the lightning. Assure them that all storms pass very quickly and that we don't have them very

often but that once the storm has passed the air is much better to breathe.

If the children do show fear of thunderstorms, teach them how to relax by lying down, closing their eyes, breathing deeply and slowly, and relaxing their limbs and muscles one by one. Help them to unwind again slowly, and give them time before they are ready to rush around again. This is a good exercise to do if a thunderstorm occurs while all the children are together, to stop any panic that may lead to mass agitation!

Wellington boots

Objective
English – to create a wet weather story book together.

Group size
Four to eight children.

What you need
Large sheets of card or sugar paper, hole punch, shoelace or wool to tie, white paper, black felt-tipped pen, coloured crayons, scissors.

Preparation
Sing the rhyme together several times and then talk about thunderstorms, what happens when it rains, what the children need to wear in the rain to stop them getting wet, what they might do in the rain. Cut the sugar paper or card to make a front and back cover for the book.

What to do
Tell the children you are going to make a book together. The book will tell the story of something that they wear in the rain. Can they guess what it is? Give them time to suggest 'wellington boots' or 'wellies'.

Let each child draw a self-portrait, showing themselves wearing clothes ready to go out in the rain, but with nothing on

their feet. Stick each portrait to a separate piece of paper, and print underneath, 'This is (*child's name*) ready to go out in the rain. But (*child's name*) has no wellington boots so (*she/he*) cannot go out!'. Help the children to 'read' the words until they can predict exactly what they are going to say.

Decide, with the children, how many pairs of wellington boots will be needed for all their pictures. Ask each child to draw and colour a pair of boots. Stick them to the next page in your book and print above the boots 'Count the boots – are there enough for everyone?'. Print below the boots 'Now we can all go out in the rain!'.

Discussion
Do the children understand what 'a pair' means? How many children are there all together? How many boots all together? But how many pairs of boots all together?

For younger children
Help them to write their names underneath their own pictures, and underneath their own pair of boots.

For older children
Extend the information by writing 'There is a pair of yellow boots for (*child's name*). A pair of red boots for (*child's name*)'.

Follow-up activities
▲ Do lightly pencilled patterns around the edges of the patterns and ask the children to trace them in thick crayon.
▲ Teach them the rhymes 'Rain, Rain, go Away', 'It's Raining, it's Pouring...', 'Incy, Wincy Spider...' and the song 'Raindrops are Falling on my Head'.
▲ Collect raindrops in different shaped bowls and dishes. Will the children collect more in a wide dish or a narrow bottle?
▲ Do photocopiable page 95 'Match the boots' to develop skills of matching and reinforce understanding of 'pairs'.

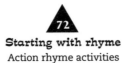

Is that thunder?

Objective
English – to make individual books describing sounds.

Group size
Three or four.

What you need
Sheets of A4 paper, scissors, pencils, crayons, sticky tape.

Preparation
Talk to the children about different loud noises. What noise do they think a clap of thunder makes? They will probably say 'Bang!'. How many more loud noises do they know? Encourage them to say the words, and remember them – for example they might have bang, clash, crack, crash, thump, toot, slam.

What to do
Each child needs a piece of paper which should be folded in half lengthways, in half the other way and then in half again. Cut along the three folds to the centre of one thickness. You now have four flaps. (If you cut the flaps slightly smaller than the back pages, the children will be encouraged to open them.)

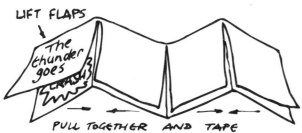

LIFT FLAPS
The thunder goes
CRASH!
PULL TOGETHER AND TAPE

Invite the children to suggest a phrase – for example 'The thunder goes crash!'. Write 'The thunder goes' on the top, and 'crash!' underneath the flap. Write some other phrases relevant to the rhyme on the other three flaps. Draw the folds together and sticky tape them to make a book.

Discussion
Talk about sounds, and invite the children to name as many sounds as they can – what does a floorboard say when it's loose? What

does a wheel do when it needs some oil? What sound does the rain make? What other weather sounds do you know?

For younger children
The cutting and folding is quite fiddly, so they will need help. Do the printing for them, but encourage them to illustrate or decorate the flaps in any way they can.

For older children
Write out the words for them to copy into their books themselves.

Follow-up activities
▲ Use this flap technique to explore other things or topics – number, colour, other sounds, and so on.
▲ Explore other ways of making sounds using percussion instruments. What can they use to make a noise like thunder?
▲ Listen to sounds – play a tape recording of simple, easily identifiable noises such as someone knocking on a door, a clock ticking, a telephone ringing, and ask the children to identify what they are.
▲ Make a picture list of all the noisy things the children can think of, in their own homes.

Running home

Objective
Mathematics – to make a spinning numbers game.

Group size
An even number of children.

What you need
Paper plate, heavy pencil or similar object, newspaper or wallpaper.

Preparation
Mark six sections on the paper plate and number each section from one – six. Put the pencil in the middle. Tear or cut the newspaper to make 'stepping stones' and lay them out to make two paths. Make sure there is an equal number of stepping stones in each path, at least 15 in each. Explain to the children that they will play in pairs, but they can all watch and wait for their turn. Help the children to choose partners.

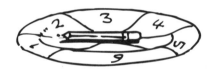

What to do
Each of the two players is allocated a path. In the game, the path is the way home. The children have to get home before the thunder begins and the rain starts to pour down. Players take turns to spin the pencil and see which number the sharpened end points to. They can step the number of squares shown, along their path.

The winner is the one who gets home first, but an exact number must be achieved to get to the end of the path.

Discussion
How can the children choose which pair will start the game, and who will go first? Can you think of a way of doing it that is fair? Can we use the numbers to help us choose? Which is the highest number out of one to six? Which is the lowest?

For younger children
They may need some help in spinning the pencil, so practise this first. Help them all to recognise the numbers one to six.

For older children
Make the paths a bit longer. Try playing three or four children at a time instead of two. Let a pair play without any supervision, show them you expect them to be responsible and not to argue.

Follow-up activities
▲ Ask the children to find different numbers of objects – one car, two blocks, three pencils, and so on.
▲ Use the words first, second, third, fourth when the children take turns, to help them learn ordinal numbers.
▲ Help the children to write the numbers one to six in sand or with chalk.

How many frogs?

Objective
Mathematics – to use thunder sounds for adding and subtracting activities.

Group size
Five or six children.

What you need
Pond and frogs from page 77, dice, a cymbal or something else with which to make a loud banging noise.

Preparation
Make the frogs and the pond. Place the pond in the middle of the table. The children each have six frogs and sit in a circle around the 'pond'. One other child has the cymbal. Sing the rhyme together. Tell the children that the cymbal is going to represent the thunder and that when the thunder makes its noise the frogs all try to get into the pond. Unfortunately they can't always all get in.

What to do
One child bangs the cymbal, the dice is rolled and the first child puts in the pond the number of frogs shown on the dice. The child bangs the cymbal again, rolls the dice and the second child puts in the correct number of frogs. Count the frogs in the pond.

Keep going round the circle. On the next round, take frogs out instead of putting them in. Count the frogs in the pond at each turn.

Discussion
Lead the children to do the adding and subtracting before they put the frogs in. If the dice shows '1' say: 'How many frogs are in the pond? How many will there be when we put one more in? How many will there be when we take one out?'.

For younger children
Limit the number of frogs to three frogs each instead of six, and put them in or take them out on every third go.

For older children
When the children can count beyond ten, use two dice instead of one and work on numbers up to twenty.

Follow-up activities
▲ Use the frogs as a stimulus for writing stories or making little frog books.
▲ Invite the children to arrange their six frogs so that they will fit underneath a sheet of A4 paper. Rub across the paper with the side of a wax crayon, to make a frog 'rubbing' picture.
▲ Talk about what other things/creatures might be found in a pond.
▲ Learn 'Five Little Speckled Frogs'.

Float or sink

Objective
Science – to chart floating and sinking experiments.

Group size
Two or three children.

What you need
Large bowl or tray for water play, water, different objects such as wood, polystyrene, brick, pebbles, paper, toy, leaf, flower, cork, ball, soap, rubber, spoon and bottle-tops. Paper, felt-tipped pen.

Preparation
Remind the children of the rhyme, and of the things they have learned about the rain. The rain makes water for us to drink, cook with, wash in and so on. What else can we do with water? Point out to the children that some things float in water, and some things sink. Do they know which things float and which sink?

What to do
Draw a chart with the following headings: Things in water/float/sink/I guess/float/sink/Am I right?

Give the children turns to put one of the items in the water tray. Let everybody guess whether the item will float or sink. Now observe what happens. Write down or draw the object in the appropriate column.

Discussion
Why do the children think some things sink and others don't? What happens to the polystyrene if you push it under and hold it down? What happens with a ball? Do the objects have to be big and heavy to make them sink? What if they're small and heavy? What if they're big and light?

For younger children
Ask them to sort the objects into floating or sinking objects before you start, then check their predictions as they go along.

For older children
Ask them to keep their own chart of 'guesses'. Show them how to tick whether they are right or wrong.

Follow-up activities
▲ Experiment with floating an egg in a bowl of tap water and then in a bowl of salt water; try the same experiment with a piece of wood.
▲ Make boats out of polystyrene – give them paper sails and sail them down a stream. What happens if you use fewer paper sails?
▲ Find out what happens if you float an ice-cube in fresh water and salty water.

Frogs in a pond

Objective
Design and Technology – to make a pond and frogs.

Group size
Three or four children.

What you need
Green card, blue card, brown card, scissors, black felt-tipped pens, adhesive.

Preparation
Sing the rhyme, 'I hear thunder'. Tell the children that frogs like to sit on the bank of the pond in the sun, or on a lily-pad, but if  they hear thunder they jump back into the pond quickly. Explain that you are going to make a frog-jumping game, first they have to make the pond and the frogs. Cut the green card into small pieces, 4cm x 2cm. Draw a large pond on the blue card, and small rocks or boulders on the brown card.

What to do
Help the children to cut out the pond and the rocks. Use the felt-tipped pen to draw some of the details in.

Give each child a piece of green card and show them how to snip the corners off at one end. Help them to make three folds in the card and to draw in two eyes and put two points for a nose. Fold the card on the creases to make the frog sit up (see the diagram below).

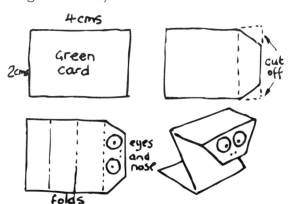

Discussion
While they're working, ask the children to tell you all they know about ponds and about frogs. Have you ever seen a frog? How big are they? What does their skin look like? Where are their eyes? What kind of noise do they make? What else lives in a pond?

For younger children
Provide plenty of support with the cutting and folding because the frogs won't balance if it goes wrong. It may be helpful to make the frogs twice as big, but you'll need a huge pond too.

For older children
Let older children cut out big round eyes to stick on to the frogs' heads, instead of drawing the eyes in.

Follow-up activities
▲ Make frog families and let the children create stories about them.
▲ Make some lily pads and lily flowers for the pond.
▲ Work on words beginning with 'f' or 'p', and words ending with 'g' and 'd'. These are difficult sounds for the children to hear, so they will need lots of repetition.

Then and now

Objective
History – to be introduced to the concepts of 'before' and 'after'.

Group size
Whole group.

What you need
Large space.

Preparation
Talk about thunderstorms and what happens during them. Invite the children to tell you anecdotes about storms. Talk about what it's like 'before' the storm (dry, hot, sometimes very oppressive) and what it's like 'after' the storm (everywhere is wet, but the sky clears and the air feels better). Tell them you are going to give them some clues and they have to decide whether you are thinking about 'before the storm' or 'after the storm'.

What to do
Sit the children in a circle and say to them, 'I'm thinking of... wet grass'. The children call out 'after the storm'. You say, 'I'm thinking of... dark clouds'. They call out 'before the storm' – and so on. Some things you might 'think' about are:
▲ looking for your umbrella;
▲ rushing home in case it rains;
▲ cars with their lights on;
▲ rumblings in the air;
▲ odd spots of rain;
▲ a rainbow;
▲ clear skies;
▲ wet pavements;
▲ soggy shoes;
▲ puddles.

Discussion
Talk about the difference between 'before' and 'after'. Can you think of other things that might have 'before' and 'after'? What about 'before Christmas' and 'after Christmas'? What about 'before your birthday' and 'after your birthday'?

For younger children
Ask younger children to concentrate on 'after the storm' and paint some rainbow pictures with them.

For older children
Let them take it in turns to be 'on', suggesting ideas for 'before' and 'after' the storm.

Follow-up activities
▲ Play the game using ideas for 'before Christmas, after Christmas', to reinforce the concept.
▲ Split a sheet of paper into three sections and ask the children to illustrate 'before, during and after the storm'.
▲ Encourage the children to tell you all the things they would need to wear to keep them dry in a rainstorm.

Which season?

Objective
Geography – to explore the environment, looking for signs of weather and seasons.

Group size
Five or six children.

What you need
Outdoor clothing suitable for the prevailing weather.

Preparation
After singing the song, talk about the weather, and ask the children if we can tell what time of year it is by the weather. As the weather is very much tied to the seasons and because 'seasons' is a very abstract concept it's a good idea to explore the environment throughout the year at different appropriate times. Get ready to go on the 'walk', helping the children to think about the things they might see.

What to do
Take a walk in your locality, looking out for any signs which tell what season it is, such as trees, plants, gardens and fields. Look out for any animals (both farm and wild).

Talk about the present season, and the other seasons and the differences that the children might see in the environment. Explain that in winter, many plants and trees lose their leaves and die away, in spring they revive and grow new leaves, in summer they grow and flower and in autumn many trees and plants have leaves that go brown and fall.

Discussion
Talk about how the children can tell if it is winter, spring, summer or autumn. Do you wear different clothes? Do you do different things? When do you play with snow? When do you go on holiday? When do the wild animals have their babies?

For younger children
Ask them to think about what the weather was like today when they were on their way to your group. Was it cold or hot, rainy or sunny? What kind of clothes are they wearing? Warm or cool? What did they wear yesterday?

For older children
Ask the children to remember what the weather was like yesterday and what they think it will be like tomorrow. Are there leaves on the trees? Are there flowers on the plants? What season do they think it is? Can they remember when the seasons seemed to change?

Follow-up activities
▲ Make a simple weather chart and help the children to set it to the appropriate picture each day.
▲ Paint pictures of snow, rainy, windy, sunny and thundery days.
▲ Use a magnifying glass to look at objects such as leaves, pebbles and twigs, found outside.
▲ Link the topic with animal habits, such as hibernation and storing food.
▲ Do photocopiable sheet 'Which will you wear?', page 96 to reinforce the activity.

▲ **79**
Starting with rhyme
Action rhyme activities

Ducks love rain

Objective
Art – to make a frieze of ducks in the rain.

Group size
Four or five children.

What you need
Blue backing paper, template of duck shape, yellow card, white card, scissors, felt-tipped pen, adhesive or sticky tape.

Preparation

Sing the rhyme together and ask the children if they can tell you a creature who loves the 'pitter patter raindrops'. If they don't guess what you mean tell them that ducks love rain. Make a simple duck-shaped template, draw around it on yellow card to provide one duck for each child. Cut out white beaks and yellow wings. Make and draw round a raindrop template several times.

What to do
Explain that they are going to make a large frieze of ducks, playing and swimming in the rain. Help the children to cut out their ducks, to stick the beaks in place and to draw in the duck's eyes. They can then cut out and stick on the wings. Help them to cut out the raindrops you have prepared.

Make the background of the frieze with blue backing paper, so that it looks like a pond. Stick the ducks to the pond. They can be swimming straight or dipping and diving. When all the ducks are on the pond, stick some raindrops at random over the frieze.

Discussion
Talk about how important it is that we have rain. Rain gives us water. Help the children to think about all the things that we need water for – to wash, to flush the toilet, to drink, to water plants and gardens, to wash clothes and so on. What do they think would happen if it didn't rain? How do people collect the rain?

For younger children
Help them to stick their own ducks on to the pond, making sure they're not all the same way round. Let them choose where to put the raindrops.

For older children
They might like to add webbed feet on to their creatures and show them dipping and diving in the pond. Help them to draw and cut out feet and stick them to their ducks.

Follow-up activities
▲ Learn the song 'Five little ducks went swimming one day...'.
▲ Give the children a very simple explanation of the rain cycle, so that they know rain comes in tiny drops from some types of cloud.
▲ Introduce a colander or sieve into water play and show the children how the drops are like the rain falling.
▲ Tip some powder paint into a puddle. Ask the children to make wellington boot footprints by stepping into the puddle and then on a sheet of paper.

Listen to the weather

Objective
Music – to make percussion instruments for rainy weather.

What you need
Yoghurt pots, empty washing-up liquid bottles, boxes, parcel tape, beans, rice, sugar, gravel, marbles, cymbals, cassette recorder.

Group size
Two or three at a time for making the instruments, then whole group to do the recording

Preparation
Sing the rhyme together and talk about how the rain sounds. Can the children describe its sound when it first begins; then as it gets louder and fiercer; then when it's really lashing down and finally as it stops? Tell the children they are going to make musical instruments so that they can 'play' a rainstorm and record it.

What to do
Divide the things you are going to put into the containers into different piles. Make sure that there are some containers with only a few of the things in, and some with a lot. For example you might have several yoghurt containers, one with only a few grains of rice in, one with twice as many, one with a huge pile. They will all make different sounds.

Fix the yoghurt pots together top to top and fasten them very carefully with strong parcel tape. Make sure all the boxes and containers are carefully fastened, so that none of the bits inside can fall out.

The shakers, when complete will all make different kinds of noises. When you are ready to begin your music making, ask the children to experiment with their shakers and decide the order in which they should perform to make a rainstorm. Use crashing cymbals to represent the thunder. Finally record the storm.

Discussion
Ask the children to decide before they begin which things will give the quietest sound, which the loudest? How can you make the rain pitter patter slowly? How can you make it really fast? How can you make the storm really build up?

For younger children
Make sure the grains, sugar and gravel cannot escape from the containers, even when they are shaken vigorously. Use plenty of parcel tape to make them secure.

For older children
Ask them to listen to each other's shakers and try to work out who should start and end the storm, how fast and how slow each shaker should be shaken, and when the thunder should sound.

Follow-up activities
▲ Draw and paint pictures of rainstorms.
▲ Tell the children about the rainforests where there is lots of rain, and about the deserts where there is hardly any.
▲ Use toothbrushes to do 'splatter' paintings.
▲ Read *Postman Pat's Rainy Day* by John Cunliffe (André Deutsch).

▲ **81**
Starting with rhyme
Action rhyme activities

Stormy weather

Objective
PE – to explore balance, shape and movement to words about weather.

Group size
Whole group.

What you need
Lots of space.

Preparation
Sing the rhyme several times, doing the actions. Encourage the children to give imaginative interpretations, ask them what the rain looks like, how it moves, how the thunder makes its noise. Encourage any kind of creative suggestion that they offer.

What to do
Beginning on the floor ask the children to slowly and quietly do 'pitter patter raindrops' with their fingers on the floor beside them. Make your voice get bigger and louder, so that they move their bodies to make heavy rain. Then make a BOOM with your voice (representing thunder). Invite them to jump up and move to the BOOM and CRASH and CRACK of your voice.

Now they can be lightning – as you go CRACK and FLASH with your voice, they can make leaps and darts and flashes, making little staccato jumps, pointing their fingers, elbows and knees. Do loud sharp hand claps for them to leap and dart to, then do fast clapping and banging to signify the rain and ask them to drum their feet upon the ground. Slowly, slowly make the rain slow down and get quieter and quieter, the storm is dying away, the children sink to the ground, the rain pitter patters on the floor again, then stops.

And then a rainbow appears. Let the children interpret the idea of the rainbow by stretching and arching.

Discussion
Ask different children to demonstrate different kinds of movement – can you leap and dart in a fast way? Can you stretch? Can you flutter? Whirl? Swivel? Stamp your

feet upon the ground? Can you be the lightning, flashing quickly? The thunder making a huge booming sound and movement? Or rumbling in the sky? Can you be the rain dying away?

For younger children
They may not know all of the words you suggest, but give praise for any imaginative shape or movement that they do. Encourage them to keep to the rhythm of your voice.

For older children
Ask them to make sounds or words to accompany their movements, making up a kind of sound poem while they're moving.

Follow-up activities
▲ Act out the story of the ugly duckling on the pond, taking shelter from the rain.
▲ Create a movement sequence, accompanied by the shakers from page 81, showing water trickling, spluttering, rushing, gushing, lashing, splishing, sploshing, dripping and plopping.
▲ Get the children to paint pictures showing how they felt when they were the rain or the running water.

Noah's ark

Objective
RE - to act out the story of the storm and Noah's ark.

Group size
Whole group.

What you need
Lots of space.

Preparation
Tell the children the story of Noah and the storm (Genesis 6–10). Noah was warned that a big storm was going to flood the earth. To save himself and his family he was to build a huge ark. On it he must get two of all the animals he could find. All the people laughed at Noah, but then the flood came, and Noah was saved. The rain went on and on. Noah sent out a little dove. It came back with an olive twig in its beak. Noah knew the storm was over. His family and the animals all came off the boat. In the sky was a glorious rainbow, this was to show God's promise to Noah that he would never flood the earth again.

What to do
First let the children act out the people's roles – Noah has just told them a storm is going to come, but they don't believe him.

Ask the children to be Noah and his family building the ark. They must collect the animals and lead them on to the ark. Some of the children can act out the animals.

The rain begins and the whole world is flooded. Ask the children to act out the parts of the family as they look out and can't see anything.

Noah sends out a dove when he thinks the storm is over. The dove comes back with a twig in its beak. The floods are gone.

Everyone leaves the ark, leading the animals out. And there, in the sky, they see a beautiful rainbow.

Discussion
Ask: Why didn't anybody listen to Noah when he told them the warning? Why did he have to take two of each animal? Which animals do you think he took? Which animals would you take? How much of the story can you remember? Which bird did Noah send to see if the storm had stopped? Why was there a rainbow?

For younger children
Help them to act the story out by themselves. Give them lots of vocal encouragement, and show them how to make the shapes of different animals. The rabbits will hop on two feet, the kittens will skip on four paws, the elephants will lumber along swinging their trunks.

For older children
Once they're familiar with the story, ask them to work in small groups, making up their own version, improvising the actions. Try and encourage each small group to perform to the rest of the group.

Follow-up activities
▲ Teach the songs 'I Can Sing a Rainbow' and 'Who Built the Ark?'
▲ Make a group story book getting the points in the story into the right sequence.
▲ Make pairs of animals, paint them and cut them out.
▲ Paint rainbows using different media.

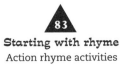

Ducks and frogs

What you need
Backing paper, scissors, sticky tape, pond and frogs from page 77 'Frogs in the pond', ducks and raindrops from 'Ducks love rain' page 80, card, felt-tipped pen, bowl or baby bath, blue frieze paper, collection of toy ducks and frogs.

Preparation
Cover the wall space with backing paper. Cut out a huge pond and stick it in the middle of the paper.

What to do
Dot the frogs around the pond sticking them on, as though they're just about to leap in. Stick the ducks on the pond. If you have dipping and diving ducks, stick them so that their tails are up. Dot the raindrops all over the frieze and stick them down with screwed-up sticky tape.

Make a heading, 'Who likes the rain? We do! shout the ducks and the frogs'. Stick the heading along the top of the display.

Write out the 'I hear thunder' rhyme in very large letters. Split the lines up and put them separately around the display, so that the children have to look for them to make the whole sequence of the rhyme.

On a small table in front of the display, put the bowl. Crumple up blue paper into it to make water and put the toy ducks on it to swim. Place the toy frogs around the 'pond'.

Discussion
Help the children to read the title of the display. Help them to look for the words of the song, and to sing them as they read. Where is your own duck? What game did we play with the frogs? Why do the ducks like the rain? How many ducks are on the pond? What colour are the ducks and frogs?

Who built the ark?

What you need
Animals from 'Noah's ark' page 83, coloured paper or fabric to make a rainbow, felt-tipped pen, backing paper, white card, brown card, green card, a few cut out and coloured figures, a white card dove with a twig in its beak.

Preparation
Back the display wall with plain paper, blue or white would be best to give a feeling of the sky.

What to do
Make the rainbow in all seven colours in an arc across one side of the display. Cut out an ark from the brown card and stick it on the display, make a landing plank leading from the ark. Attach the animals, two-by-two, coming down the landing plank, out of the ark. Stick the figures on to represent Noah's family. Put the dove in the sky.

Make a heading on the white card, 'The story of Noah's Ark' and stick it at the top of the display. Write labels saying:
Look for the animals.
What colours are in the rainbow?
Where is the dove?
When the flood came, Noah built an ark.
Noah saved the animals.
When the rain stopped, there was a rainbow in the sky.

Discussion
Go through the sequence of the story. Encourage the children to tell you what is happening on different parts of the display. Tell me the story in your own words and try to name all the animals. Help them to 'read' the words – can you see the word 'Noah'?

Pitter patter raindrops

Group size
Five or six children.

What you need
225g icing sugar, peppermint essence, a knob of butter/margarine, knife, wooden spoon, bowl, flour, large plate/baking tray, sieve.

Preparation
Assemble all the ingredients and equipment. Sprinkle some flour on your surface. Make sure the children have clean hands and are wearing a clean apron.

What to do
Sift the icing sugar into a bowl. Chop up your knob of butter carefully with a knife and put it into the bowl. Add a few drops of peppermint essence. Cream the icing sugar and butter together to form a stiff mixture. If it is too soft, add some extra icing sugar.

Give each child a teaspoonful of the mixture and ask them to make it into a small ball. Help them to use the knife to make a raindrop shape 'sweet'

Put the sweets on to the tray or plate and leave them to harden for a while. If the children do not like peppermint you could use a different flavour.

Discussion
Ask the children why they think they need to use a sieve at the beginning. What should they do if the mixture isn't thick enough?

Follow-up activities
▲ Use this sweet recipe to make different coloured raindrops, by adding a drop of food colouring. Experiment with different colours and flavours.
▲ Use the sweets for counting – how many will they need to make for one each?

Making tea

Colour, cut and stick.

Can you put these pictures in the right order to make a cup of tea?

Stir in the milk.

Fill the kettle.

Put in the teabags.

Drink the tea.

Pour the tea.

Fill the teapot with water.

Which teapots match?

Starting with rhyme
Action rhyme activities

Label the parts

How many parts can you label?

head	arm	hand	toe
eye	finger	leg	hair
mouth	elbow	knee	trunk

89

Starting with rhyme
Action rhyme activities

photocopiable ▶ **activities** ◀

What do you know?

Colour the picture.

Can you see:

⌒ a hill?

〰 a river?

⬡ a bridge?

🏠 houses?

🏫 a school?

**Tick in the boxes
when you have
seen them.**

〰 a road?

🌳 a wood?

Starting with rhyme
Action rhyme activities

photocopiable
▶ **activities** ◀

How many cakes?

Draw one more in each set.

How many in each set?

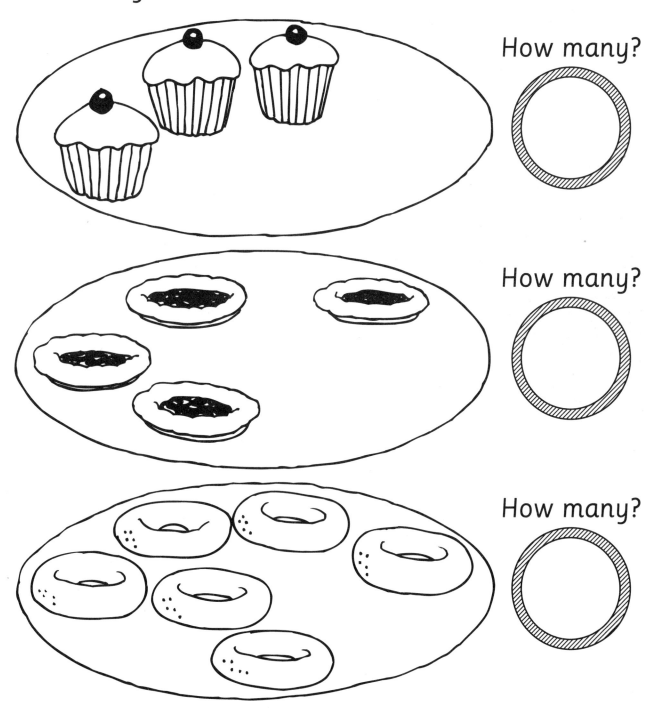

How many?

How many?

How many?

Which is the biggest set?

Which is the smallest set?

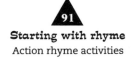

91

Starting with rhyme

Action rhyme activities

Follow the paths

Make a path of your own.

photocopiable ▶ **activities** ◀

Who's on the bus?

Who says what:

driver

sit down nicely

mums

rah, rah, rah

move down the bus

dads

teacher

doze, doze, doze

children

chatter, chatter, chatter

Make up some more of your own. What do they say?

93

Starting with rhyme
Action rhyme activities

Match the wheels

Draw a zigzag pathway to the wheels that match.

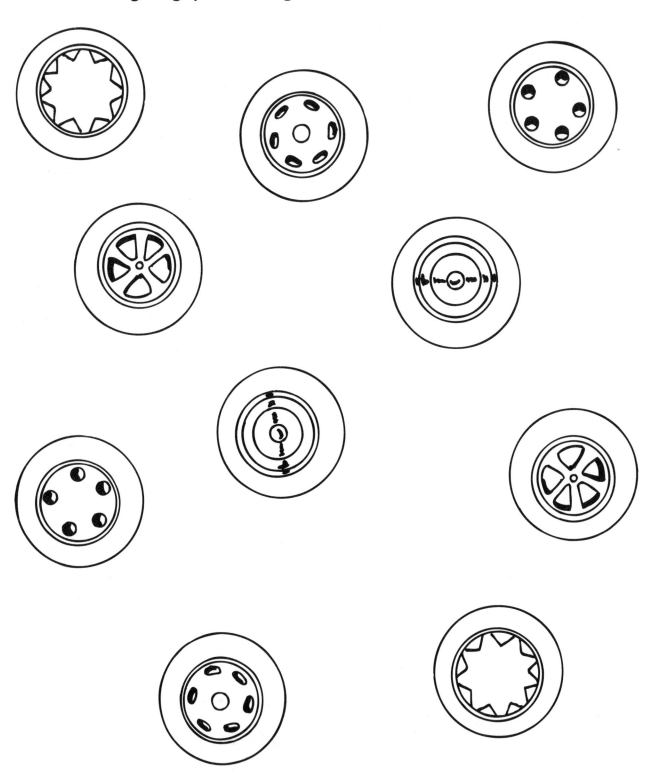

Colour the wheels. Colour the pairs the same.

Match the pairs

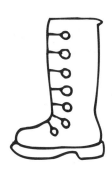

How many boots?

How many pairs?

Colour each pair.

Starting with rhyme

Action rhyme activities

Which clothes will you wear?

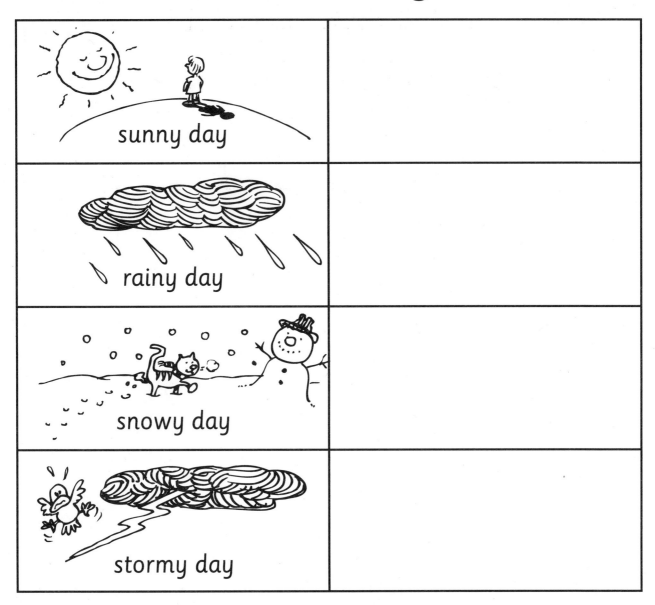

Colour, cut and stick. Choose from:

Starting with rhyme
Action rhyme activities